She

(BELIEVED SHE COULD SO SHE DID)

STORIES & IMAGES BY

Deborah Cole

Printed in the United States of America
First Printing, 2021
ISBN 978-1-954479-00-5
Positively Powered Publications
PO Box 270098
Louisville, CO 80027
PositivelyPoweredPublications.com
Cover design and Interior layout by Victoria Wolf, wolfdesignandmarketing.com.
Author photo by Carmen Davailus
Photo copyrights by Deborah Cole unless otherwise stated.
Author website: www.deborahcoleconnections.com

Contents

Part 1: She Believed She Could

Part 2: So She Did

Jessica Gardner McCoy

Carmaleta McKinnis-Williams

Aditi Merchant

Wanda Montemayor

Chi Ndika

Lorie Newman

Katarzyna Priebe

Veronica Schnitzius

Joy Selak

Cassie Shankman

Marcia Silverberg

Lisa Webb

Carolyn Simpson Wells

Dr. Aisha White

Dr. Angie Whitworth

Vanessa Wilkerson

Diana Zuniga

Resources
Gratitude

PART 1:

She Believed
She Could

Be a Lady, They Said

"WE CANNOT CHANGE WHAT WE ARE NOT AWARE OF, AND ONCE WE ARE AWARE, WE CANNOT HELP BUT CHANGE."

—SHERYL SANDBERG

"*Be a lady.*" This message was loud and clear from an early age. I cannot recall what any of the circumstances might have been, but if I heard this once, I heard it said a thousand times during my growing-up years. I had tucked it way back in the memory bank of annoying and/ or nagging things that were said to me as a child. In fact, I hadn't even thought of it peripherally until recent months when I read a blog post by Camille Rainville (aka Writings of a Furious Woman) with that title. Reading her words was like being hit with the proverbial ton of painful and emotional bricks. *Be a lady.* I had not heard that phrase for decades, but the reading of it sent me into a painful spiral of unworthiness. You know the one. Where your happy and confident self is suddenly sent into a dark place of remembering and believing you are not enough and will never be enough.

Rainville's somewhat lengthy blog post hit all of those buttons, long since forgotten yet still sensitive. As children, our ideas of who we are can be bolstered or demolished by those around us whose words have power. Parents, relatives, siblings, teachers and friends all help to either confirm or deny how we feel about ourselves. As little girls trying to sort out meaning from the mystery, self-worth can be sent soaring or dashed

against the rocks. *Be a lady.* This phrase and, in fact, any statement like "Be x or y or z" implies that the listener is *not* x or y or z and that there are guidelines and rules to follow to become that. As children, all we have are the words and actions of those around us to reinforce our place in society and in the world. And we tend to believe those who have power over us. We think the "big" people have all the answers and know all the rules. And we listen. And listen.

Be a lady. Is being a lady the ultimate in perfection of who I want to become? Are the actions and activities involved in being a lady in agreement with how we see ourselves as young girls/women? And frankly, what exactly does being a lady mean? To top it all off, I grew up in the South and without many financial resources. In the humorous book "Southern Ladies and Gentlemen," originally published in 1975, Florence King writes about how, as Southerners, women (and men) are supposed to act. I read this book soon after it was launched and laughed through it, while feeling the pinch of truth in the expectations of little Southern girls. The book, albeit funny, was somewhat embarrassing. Could it be because I saw a shred of truth in the writing? The author's description of the possibility of self-rejuvenating virginity is laughable, but as a Southern girl, I understand. The author's statement, "A lady is required to be frigid, passionate, sweet, bitchy and scatterbrained all at the same time. Her problems spring from the fact that she succeeds," now makes me wince. To think that these attitudes existed (and still exist) is pretty painful. And to think that some of the standards of proper Southern lady behavior, which are so humorously described, are still in full-blown execution today is shocking.

Be a lady. Do this, don't do that, think this way, say this, look like this, don't look like that, what will others say, what will so-and-so think, follow this recipe and you will be that pinnacle of all-glorious deities … a lady. I hope not to be misunderstood in this rant on ladylike behavior. I respect many of the attributes ascribed to ladies (and gentlemen as well), such as kindness, compassion, concern for others and friendliness. But some of the unwritten rules don't work any longer, including hiding your true feelings, shunning your own needs, living the life of a centuries-old model for ladylike behavior because your great-grandmothers/fathers acted this way, and doing it without question or consideration of self. Generations of unhappy people, with unfulfilled dreams and aspirations, are left languishing on the sidelines of life when women aspire to be ladies and men struggle to be gentlemen. The prescriptions for success in those two categories are outdated and should be left in the past.

Be a lady. Ladies act in certain ways. Ladies look a certain way. Ladies are never too showy, never too smart, never better than others. They are always polite, always put everyone else first and always good at only ladylike things. And if you don't or can't, if all else fails, hide it or reject it. What if these rules don't fit (and I'm here to say they often do not)? What if what we are meant to do, be or say simply does not fall into the category of what the *Be a lady* advocate intends?

In the past, women and men were out of luck. There were few avenues for being different and not toeing the line of proper behavior. Being perfect without being too obvious about it set girls and women up for massive disappointment. But that was the past, and this is the now.

Living a life of "doing the right thing" and fitting into someone else's mold is neither satisfying nor purposeful. We occupy our place on earth for such a short period of time, and we are in this incarnation for a reason. Most often, we do not know that purpose for many years, and it finds us before we find it. This discovery of life's purpose might involve not merely uncovering what we might become, but also peeling off layers of notions about ourselves—notions that do not serve us toward that end goal. In a section of "Be a Lady They Said," Rainville writes,

> "Be a lady they said. Don't talk too loud. Don't talk too much. Don't take up space. Don't sit like that. Don't stand like that. Don't be intimidating. Why are you so miserable? Don't be a bitch. Don't be so bossy. Don't be assertive. Don't overact. Don't be so emotional. Don't cry. Don't yell. Don't swear. Be passive. Be obedient. Endure the pain. Be pleasing. Don't complain. Let him down easy. Boost his ego. Make him fall for you. Men want what they can't have. Don't give yourself away. Make him work for it. Men love the chase. Fold his clothes. Cook his dinner. Keep him happy. That's a woman's job. You'll make a good wife someday. Take his last name. You hyphenated your name? Crazy feminist. Give him children. You don't want children? You will someday. You'll change your mind."

How I remember all of these admonitions. Don't talk too loudly. Don't talk too much. Don't be full of yourself. Being too outspoken or saying what you think or feel are simply not the marks of a lady.

Be a lady. Some admonitions are good and have merit: "Be safe. Watch out for harm. Don't be out too late. Don't act inappropriately." But their intention is not because we should value our own wellness and safety but that if we head down the sketchy path, we will not be seen as ladylike. A lot of "don'ts" fulfill the goal of being a lady.

Be a lady. I now see that the love for our brothers and sisters on earth (as long as they were the "right" brothers and sisters) was an unspoken and very wrong message. It goes without saying that compassion and consideration of others are important. But at what cost to ourselves? Prioritizing others in our thinking, being and doing because it leads to acceptance as a lady or gentleman—these messages are without merit.

It was quite confusing as a little girl. I had many questions with no answers. The reminders to *be a lady* always seemed to come at a time when I was having fun and/or following my natural inclinations. Did being a lady mean I shouldn't be too loud or too quiet but just the perfectly curated decibel level? Lesson learned. I could be bubbly and outgoing with friends at school (this often resulted in "talks too much" on my report cards), but at home, where ladylike attitudes were valued, being quiet was most important. Being curious, questioning and eager to learn new things were a part of my uncelebrated life outside my family. These did not fall into the ladylike column. As the younger sister of a brother five years my senior, I

saw and perceived differences in how we were treated. Some activities and attitudes were acceptable for my brother but not for me. Young children learn quickly how they receive praise and how they receive corrective direction. I realized that my brother, who played baseball, and my dad, who coached it, were the perfect combination that the family celebrated. So, I created a girls' softball team.

I organized the girls, gathered up equipment and the girls showed up, but my dad did not. He was a loving dad but not a supporter of activities that fell out of the scope of molding my "lady skills." He had a plausible reason for not making the practice, but I recognized that a girls' team was never going to happen.

Be a lady. We all need role models and mentors as we learn new things. The admonition to act like a lady came from my dad, and the role model he always (not in so many words) set on the pedestal was his mother. She was an amazing grandmother with lots of love and affection for all four grandchildren, especially for the sole granddaughter—me. If being a lady meant a lot of "don'ts," the "do's" came from watching how my grandmother conducted herself. She was a true Southern lady. She was a good cook, a great seamstress, active socially with lots of lady friends, impeccably dressed and the one who introduced me to drinking tea. Attending a tea or drinking tea were prime examples of how ladies acted. Long before my time, most ladies drank tea wearing hats, gloves and girdles. I was exposed to these trappings at an early age and came to realize that if I wanted to *be a lady*, I needed to conduct myself (and dress) like my grandmother. I was moldable and compliant. Becoming a lady? Yes please, if that yielded approval and acceptance in the world of adults I knew best.

Be a lady. And let's go shopping. Who wouldn't say yes to this? As a child, I received two pairs of shoes (one in the fall for the start of school and a new pair of nice shoes at Easter) and six dresses per year. I was ecstatic to be invited by Grandmother to go shopping for something new to wear to an upcoming event packed with adults. I was putty in her ladylike hands. At the end of the day, my 12-year-old self had a new dress in a goldish-green-ish color with a dark green ribbon around the bodice (bodice is a very ladylike term for breast coverings), a pair of very uncomfortable pointy black shoes, a white hat and white gloves *and* the ultimate of all ladylike possessions—a pair of hose and a girdle. What the heck was a 12-year-old girl doing in a girdle? Yes, it was needed to hold up the hose (on my unshaven, hairy girl legs), but more to the point, this was the uniform of a lady. I do not remember many events from childhood other than feelings and a few occasions, but I do remember my grandmother giving me the instructions that I should always wear a girdle in public situations because to be without one was just "slouchy." I loved my grandmother deeply, but the message that was etched into my brain was that without said restrictive garment, I would always be slouchy. Sigh.

I do not fault myself for not having the chutzpah to stand up for myself. This was how I was raised from a young age. *Be a lady*. Act like a lady. Do the things that ladies do (and this list is narrow). The voice in my head hammered home what was expected. As a child, my power was in others' hands and would stay there until, little by little, I began to redefine how living a purposeful and successful life might unfold. The unfolding did not come in one brilliant flash of light or major aha moment but rather in the acceptance of how things could be, how alternatives to being ladylike could also be satisfying while doing no harm to others.

Everyone develops and uncovers purpose and fulfillment at their own pace. I believe that today's young women can be all that they want to be, do all that they want to do and do so with the approval and acceptance of their families and support systems. Times have changed. Above all, *Be a lady* has morphed into "You can be whatever you want to be. And while you are accomplishing this, be kind and give it your all. We love you no matter what." Words as well as actions support women in their growth and development. Outward appearances are no longer the gold standard for how to grow up and mature into a fully functioning, happy individual. Are we completely there yet? No. The world still portrays women as "acceptable" according to body image, grooming, and adherence to female norms. But we have come a long way, baby!

Peeling the Onion

"IF YOU DON'T CHALLENGE YOURSELF,
YOU WILL NEVER REALIZE WHAT
YOU CAN BECOME."

—ANONYMOUS

As I became acutely aware that "being a lady" wasn't an easy role for me (at least the hat, gloves and girdle get-up), I began to stretch my wings ever so slightly. As I moved through high school toward graduation, I had no idea where my life would take me or what path I should choose. I knew what I liked, such as being out-of-doors, science, history, projects and planning, but in those days, advising young women how to harness their likes and dislikes was not in the scope of high school counselors or parents. I felt that I was shuffling along toward who-knows-what, listening to the covert and occasionally overt suggestions that guided my interests. There were no discussions of what college might serve me best, and now I understand why. My parents had only finished high school, and college was a foreign concept.

When, in a fit of frustration, I tossed out the idea that I might just skip college and find a job, my parents were supportive. What? I had no skills, no goals and no grand plan for diving into a long-held dream. I think at the time I was testing their interest in my education. Fortunately, I took charge of my plans and chose a school that I believed they could afford (a major consideration at the time). We were at the tail end of the days (pre-women's movement) when finding a husband and making a home were high on the list of goals for most women. No one ever asked me what my professional interests might be. And I mean no one.

I now cringe to think that these were the ways of guidance. My personal interests of being involved in nature and the environment were never mentioned or considered in career choices. And the word "career" was not a part of educational discussions. Ouch. With a bit of compassion now under my belt as a parent, I understand the lack. My parents had no education beyond high school, and they had jobs, not careers. My wonderful parents guided me with the knowledge and understanding that they had, and I do not fault them for it.

When I took a summer job as a data processor after high school (in the medieval times of the 1960s this was labeled a key punch operator) in order to earn college spending money, I saw that the group of women who filled these roles appeared less than happy, even bordering on grumpy. They didn't like the job, the firm, the work, their husbands/family or much of anything. Not a lot of joy or hope or prospects for it. But I was aware of a group of people called programmers who floated in and out of the computer room (back in those days, the IBM 360 was housed in a big room). They seemed focused and serious, yet cheerful and motivated. All that being said, the two groups of people (women in key punch and men in programming) never interacted. The programmers were described in awe-filled commentaries as the elite. Although I had trained (at my dad's urging) to be one of the women in the data entry field, I believed it would be much more intriguing to be one of those who seemed to be highly motivated and enthusiastic about their work and profession.

As a freshman, I learned that there was, in fact, a degree in computer science. Not having any notion of what direction I wanted to go in college, I believed this would be intriguing and fulfilling. And it was. Everything about it appealed to me: the problem-solving, the hands-on manipulation of that gargantuan IBM 360 that filled a large room and the mystery of how to move from problem to solution using a human brain in alignment with a machine. All were my cup of tea. I loved it, and I thrived. Upon graduation, I married and also landed a job as an entry-level programmer for a startup in Dallas. The hours were long and demanding. A bit of travel was also involved. Although the work and the challenge appealed to me in every way, I could not say the same for my family. My husband was resentful, and my parents not supportive. All urged me to leave the company, which I chose not to do. I was fulfilled there, earning a good salary and learning a lot.

When my husband chose to take his life, my world shifted. At a young age, I was a widow, unsure how to navigate this new personal role and with no "adults" to mentor or support me in this maelstrom of confusion. And again I was urged to leave the company. I chose to stay, but then the company downsized, and I was let go, suddenly without what had been feeding me literally as well as figuratively.

Who could I look to for support? The family who had pressured me to give up what I felt to be a strong calling? Did I have any role models to emulate? None that I could see. Many of my friends had taken the predictable route of marrying, having children and doing what I had subconsciously known was the "right" thing. But here I was in a situation never planned, never expected and with so many loose ends that even a complex program could not resolve them all.

If my family wasn't supportive of my purpose or profession, I would live out my choices at a distance. I moved away to restart my education and get a degree in education. This would be an acceptable purpose, right? But it did not inspire me or excite me in any way. After graduating with a degree in education, specializing in biology and history, I again landed a job as a programmer, this time in a service agency that was eager to grow a new segment fueled by a cadre of entry-level programmers. I enjoyed it there, but after two years, there was a mass layoff, and again I was left to discern my direction.

Throughout the second programming job, I had continued to take classes at the University of Texas. The classes were all science, primarily in the botany department. I had always held a fierce love of nature, whether it was camping as part of the Girl Scouts or as a home gardener from an early age. Being outdoors not only appealed to me, but it healed me. I had to largely ignore this tug at my soul since my work as a computer geek had to be accomplished indoors (during that time).

I never once asked myself, "What feeds my soul?" or "How can I serve others through living out my purpose?" Introspection was not in my lexicon. I listened to the nagging voice in my head that always told me to do something that would be acceptable to those around me. *Be a lady,* they said. Although they didn't use those words—words I'd heard so frequently so long ago—the sense of the message was the same.

At the point where I had completed my second degree and was then laid off from my job as a programmer, I decided to do what felt right for me. Because I knew that all of my coursework in science and botany could get me out-of-doors, I investigated professions and degrees in a field that would be just right for me. I discovered a master's program at Texas A&M University that would allow me to gain knowledge as well as experience in areas I loved—the outdoors and science—all wrapped up in a program called Landscape Horticulture. The self-discovery continued. This time it took a fair amount of conversation with my parents to explain yet another degree, a move to another city and another goal. Beyond love and emotional support, I asked nothing of them, as I had been self-supporting for several years.

In my world, growing up and getting married was always one of the boxes a lady checked off. This achievement received the ultimate approval rating. Again, I do not fault my family for believing this. It was what was important in their time. Safety, security and stability (and happiness?) for a woman came in the form of a man with a good means for earning a living and therefore taking care of his wife and family. The notion that a woman might strike out on her own, be independent, manage her own life, live out her own mission and purpose … these were not a part of my understanding or that of my parents and family.

On several occasions, I questioned my beliefs. Although I had long ago internalized the idea that my highest calling was to find a husband, I felt that possibly I was simply not meant to be married, or at least that this should not be my primary goal. I was too cantankerous, too unladylike, too unconventional, too *something* that did not fit the mold of how I was raised. Yet time and time again, I gave in and listened to the voice in my head that caused me to doubt. And so marry again I did.

I was fortunate in that my new husband did not have expectations of a Southern lady who would be happy to cook, rear children, do lunch and manage the home. He had his own career to pursue, and as long as my endeavors did not interfere with his, I was left to my own devices. Following graduation from Texas A&M, I was hired by a state agency to oversee some of the public grounds. I earned a minimum wage but was happy and remained in that post until I had a baby and took some time off to be with her. When she was two and I wanted to move back into the workforce in perhaps a more challenging role, I was presented with a new opportunity. I was hired by the public schools to teach a one-year vocational horticulture program, and I enjoyed every minute of it. At the end of the contract, I was offered the opportunity to move to a high school and teach biology and physics; however, this felt like moving backward. Teaching was "acceptable" and approved as a profession for a woman, but something was missing—something large—and that was the passion for getting up each morning and giving it 1,000% of my efforts. I enjoyed the students, but public education was at a difficult point of integration, segregation and how to make it all work.

The days seemed to be spent in bureaucracy and administrative duties rather than in teaching.

During the summer before my potential transfer to a high school teaching position, a close friend who was a landscape architect asked me if I would become a partner with her in a landscape business. The idea of spending my days outdoors, working creatively and productively to beautify our local environment, was intriguing. But I had questions. Would we earn enough money to support a business or ourselves? How would we do it? How would we find work? I knew nothing about running a business. I asked all of the "who?" and "how?" questions but failed to ask the most important question, which was "*why?*"

Was it possible to reconcile working in an environment that wasn't typically what "my people" did? Yes, in past generations, they had been farmers, but that was to supply their families with food. It wasn't to earn a living, and it certainly was not pursued by women except in support roles. Design, build and maintain landscapes? It was what I had been trained for and knew, but I had never, and I mean *never,* planned to pursue my love of landscape as part of a business I owned. And when I shared with my parents that I was leaving a teaching job with insurance, benefits and a title that they understood and knew to be appropriate for a woman, my mother lovingly said, "Are you sure you want to do that?" Hell no, I wasn't sure, but I was eager to be everything that I could be and accept responsibility and accountability for the success and/or failure of everything that happened. I was ready to *love* and live my purpose.

I imagined freedom, creativity, discovery, fulfillment and, above all, making a difference in the lives of those we served. Not very lofty goals for many, but big ones for me. I never saw the path to entrepreneurship as a way to become incredibly wealthy, except in personal fulfillment and arriving at a place where I could support the needs of others as well as myself. And to do it all in an environment that made my heart sing—out-of-doors. We opened our doors for business on October 16, 1981, as Greater Texas Landscapes, Inc.

It is impossible to describe the feelings of that first day of this new reality. With each action and each decision, I felt a sense of freedom and a feeling of being "complete" that I had never before experienced. I also felt fear, concern, gratitude, worry, joy and a deep, deep awareness of destiny playing out as it should.

Was I prepared for this wild ride of entrepreneurship? One might say I was not equipped in a traditional sense. I had no formal business education and no capital other than a $1,000 teacher retirement plan that I cashed in. I had no apprenticeship or training and no mentors or role models. But what I did have was a love of the field of study and a love of the out-of-doors. Even greater than the feel-good aspects of this venture was the possibility of creating a business that would be a reflection of me and my values and fulfill my underlying desire to be of service.

For the first time in my life, I felt like I was really bucking the system. I gave up a traditional job in a traditional setting with a regular salary and benefits and all of the things that a working person aspires to claim for their own. And I entered the world of working from home for long hours with no extra compensation and wearing a uniform of a T-shirt, jeans and boots. What was I thinking? I was deliriously happy.

At the time, there was one other landscape company of any size in our hometown of Austin, Texas, and it was owned by two men. I sought them out to ask questions and to learn from them. Helping others to learn and get ahead was a part of my nature, and I assumed that to be the case for other people as well. Little did I realize that even though my business partner and I were very small potatoes, we were seen as a threat. Only later did I learn that part of the reason one of the competitor partners was willing to visit with us was because he had a romantic interest in my partner. I was a bit naïve. But ask I did.

My curiosity to find out how to make this fledgling operation run led me to taking classes in business accounting and marketing, and joining workshops by professional organizations in operations and planning. After adding a small maintenance division to our services, I enrolled in a lawn mower repair class to understand their purchase and repair. Each time I was presented with a new question or issue to resolve, I looked to those who could educate me. After a few years of leasing small construction equipment, I determined it would be most economical to purchase a skid-steer loader. I then enrolled in a course to learn how to use, maintain and operate loaders.

Why all of this ongoing education and training? Because I knew what I didn't know and believed that by becoming well-educated, I could better serve my company, my staff and my clients. I believed I could, so I did, and I didn't hesitate for a moment. My reluctance to embrace how I wanted to live and what I wanted to do was over. I became aware of why, what and how I wanted to live out my purpose.

My business partner and I grew the business with many ups and downs along the way, and they always led to bigger ups and bigger opportunities.

I am so very grateful for her friendship and for our ability to work through all of those initial mysteries of business ownership. She left the business after three years to marry and move out of state. At the time of her departure, I had to do some heavy questioning of myself and my abilities. The business was growing. Could I do it alone? Did I have the moxie to be the "one at the top" responsible for everything that went right … and wrong? The answer was yes. I would no longer look to others to make the magic happen. Until this time, I had not become aware of the importance of "growing up," not only the business and myself, but others. Yes, I was ultimately responsible for everything that occurred in the organization, but now I woke up to the fact that supporting others in their growth and fulfilling their dreams (as I had *not* been) was crucial. Standing beside others in their professional path to achieving their dreams was my focus.

When my business partner left, we had a staff of a dozen or so people. We were involved in landscape design, construction and maintenance not only for residences but also for commercial developments. Looking back, it is hard to know how we achieved all that we achieved, but I do know I worked long hours. Seven days was a typical work week, and I felt it was important to be present from the time the gate was unlocked in the morning until we closed at night. We continued to grow. We continued to count our successes, including projects that earned state and national awards for our construction and maintenance work. I was proud of the business, the staff and myself. Over the 35 years as head of the company, I helped the business make many industry friends and developed many careers. I have no regrets.

As Greater Texas Landscapes grew to over 200 employees in three offices, I believed it was my responsibility to ensure the future of the business through an exit strategy that would benefit the employees who had worked so hard to grow the company. After a lot of research, discussions and planning, I sold my shares of stock to an existing employee-owned landscape company of similar philosophy and culture. In this way, I knew that should I be hit by the infamous mystery truck, the future of the company would be secure. Jobs for my most beloved employees would be safe. We merged our companies in 2008, and I was comfortable that the future of the company I had founded was protected. I remained with the combined companies, expanded our footprint to 10 locations, increased staff to nearly 500 and improved our sales to reach top 20 status in the nation.

I am most proud of the company for providing paths for growth and development for so many individuals. The opportunities we provided for the entire workforce were second to none. I watched as new hires who had an enthusiasm to learn and get ahead did just that. My mission to provide the best quality service through landscape construction and maintenance was just as important as my mission to inspire hope so that others could realize their potential. We did it!

At Last

In leaving a company I loved, a profession that I adored and a staff that I could not imagine life without, I faced some serious personal backlash. Who was I, if not a business owner? How could I possibly fill each day without such comradery? It had taken me far too long to unravel all of my childhood beliefs and erroneous thinking, and now I had chosen to start again? Yes, I had. And how could I continue to support others in their journeys to professional fulfillment, and celebrate their successes, in a world or family situation that sometimes didn't support their dreams? I wanted to learn, and not just from nationally well-known figures, but from women like me who were working through their beliefs, right or wrong. I knew that thousands of women were being educated, seeking training and carrying big personal loads in order to fulfill their dreams of creating their own paths to success.

I wanted to understand where women were positioned in the workplace and knew this called for numbers. Who doesn't love statistics? I learned at an early age that in preparing for any significant discussion, you can always find statistics to support a claim. And statistics indicate that women in business, women as owners and women as innovators or founders are becoming more abundant. We know with certainty that women, as well as men, own businesses; however, attitudes have been slow to change. Ask an adult or child to describe a business owner, and often they will mention a man. Men are in the news every day. Apple, Amazon, Google and Microsoft all have male founders. Most lists of top business owners/entrepreneurs in America list all males with the exception of one female, Oprah Winfrey.

When teens were asked to name entrepreneurs who inspire them, only 49% of the young men and 33% of the young women could think of someone. Of the names mentioned, 85% were men, and 15% were women. The most-named person was Kylie Jenner. Clearly, we have a ways to go. Surveys indicate that in past years, there might have been a lack of relatable role models.

We know that women do create, own and run businesses. And there is hope for even greater progress now and in the future. Whereas in the past, women-owned businesses in the U.S. were a fraction of the total number, as of 2021, 40% of all U.S. businesses are women-owned and approach 12.3 million in number. Sixty-four percent of all new women-owned businesses in 2020 were started by women of color, and Latina women-owned businesses grew by more than 87%. And the best news of all? Today there are 114% more women entrepreneurs than there were in the year 2000.

And then there are the financial numbers to consider. Only 25% of women business owners seek financing from outside interests. Instead, they are either bootstrapping the new operation or receiving assistance from family and friends. Women receive just 7% of the total venture capital for their startups for various reasons, but this number, too, is changing. When they do seek financing, female entrepreneurs ask for approximately $35,000 less than men ask for. Some of the best news of all is that women-founded companies often outperform male-owned companies financially, creatively and in employee retention.

Women from ages 18 to over 65 were asked why they started their businesses when they did. The women noted an open opportunity, passion, a job change, experience and education in their chosen field, family considerations, and necessities such as layoffs and looking for extra income.

When comparing the women's ages and the reasons they opened a new business, two points stand out in the data. Twenty-eight percent of business owners under age 34 started a business based on seeing an opportunity in the market, and 28% of owners over age 65 started a business out of necessity.

When asked to elaborate on her reason for starting a business based on opportunity, one millennial in a national study said, "I had an idea and decided it was the time to build it." Meanwhile, one baby boomer who started her business out of necessity shared, "I was going to be laid off from a job of 22 years with no pension." Aside from opportunity and necessity, the next-highest reason women opened a business was family considerations for both the 35-44 (23%) and the 45-54 (26%) age bracket. Family considerations took different forms. One woman in this category said, "It coincided with when we decided to start our family." Another said, "I rushed into my business because I didn't have children." Both shared very different family-driven reasons for starting their businesses.

Armed with some facts and figures, I set out to find, interview, photograph and introduce the world to a sample of the thousands of brave women who create businesses and stand up as role models for the future of all young girls. No longer do we have our lives mapped out for us by the expectations of others. No longer do we need to gain approval from others for doing whatever we have determined is the "right thing" for us. We can (and do) chart our own paths and have control over fulfilling our life's purposes.

The 35 women you will meet in this book are only a small sample of all the courageous, dedicated, smart and wonderful women who make up that 40% of business owners. It is encouraging to know how many females are now in leadership roles in our country and how many women have a seat at the table in decision-making. Not only does business culture have to be attuned to this shift, but also we as women have to embrace the knowledge that we are capable. We are able to provide the kind of guidance that we need in a world where compassionate leadership may be in the minority. I am very proud to share these 35 women with the world. They are out there every day doing what they do best. They include women who are single, with families, in business for many years or just starting out. Their ages span five decades, and they come from wide-ranging backgrounds. They have inspiring stories to tell and lead incredible, courageous lives. I am proud of them and the thousands of other women they represent. They are us, and they are our role models for future generations. These women believed they could, so they did.

PART 2:

So She Did

Alta

ALEXANDER

Altatudes

The definition of "tough cookie" is someone who is resilient and able to rebound after tough times. Alta Alexander is not only a brilliant, witty and warm individual, but those who know her say her name should follow the definition of "tough cookie" in the dictionary. She is a remarkable role model for resilience, and her journey in business affirms this.

Alta is the owner of a Altatudes, a boutique located in the heart of historic East Austin, Texas. The shop features high-end women's apparel and accessories from over 25 international labels, as well as some brands that call Austin their home. She carefully curates all of the items in the shop. This was the vision of Alta, the high energy boutique owner who was on track to success. Then 2020 changed the course of business.

Alta grew up in Smithville, Texas, but has lived in Austin since she was 12. She graduated from Huston-Tillotson University, earning a bachelor's degree in business and communications. Prior to opening her boutique, she worked for tech and media companies, as well as gaining significant retail experience in upscale boutiques and large national chains. With her experience in business and retail, after several years Alta was able to realize a lifelong dream of having her own business, fueled by her supportive husband's gift of funds to cover startup rent. He was and is one of her biggest fans.

SHE *Alta*

As a youngster, Alta was encouraged by her grandmother to dream big and always push through her fear. When starting a business, fear can be huge. It can be caused by feelings of not knowing where to start, not being expert at everything, being considered foolish to leave a "good job," not having enough capital and not attracting customers. The concerns are numerous. Alta was well prepared for unanticipated challenges, which are inevitable in the life of an entrepreneur.

SHE *alta*

She opened her boutique in 2017 as "the first Black-owned upscale womenswear boutique in Austin," utilizing personal savings so that she did not have to seek bank financing. Her vision was to someday bring her grandchildren into the operation. Alta intentionally selected her location in an East Austin neighborhood that had been experiencing revitalization in the past decade. She remembers visiting the location as a young child when it housed Zodiac Records. Supporting the neighborhood and the Black community, where she is extremely active, is important to Alta. She is a member of Leadership Austin, Austin Area Urban League, Austin Chamber of Commerce, Austin Women's Chamber of Commerce, Greater Austin Black Chamber of Commerce and the Austin branch of the NAACP. In addition, she is a charter member and past officer of the Lone Star Chapter of The Links. One of her proudest positions is serving as the president of the East 12th Street Merchants Association, where she provides advice and service to her fellow retailers in the area.

2020 began on a very positive note for Alta and Altatudes. The boutique was thriving, and customers came to appreciate her for her inventory as well as her fashion sense. First, the onset of the COVID-19 pandemic caused her shop to temporarily close, which was a blow. She and many of her fellow retailers applied for Paycheck Protection Program (PPP) loans when news of federal assistance was announced. They were all denied without explanation. But she held on. And then early in the morning of June 7 of that year, a fire began in the adjoining space, resulting in smoke and water damage to her entire inventory. Her shop, which had reopened with new COVID-19 guidelines, was closed again. In true community fashion, those who knew and loved Alta came to her rescue for immediate needs. A GoFundMe campaign (split between the two affected businesses) put together by friends helped with initial expenses, followed by an individual GoFundMe account to assist Alta. She is also deeply grateful to the members of the local chapter of The Links who came to her aid to not only inventory her merchandise for insurance purposes, but also to get out and get their hands dirty helping with the cleanup and disposal of all of her clothing and accessories.

This assistance received in a time of need helped ease the pain of the tragedy. Although Alta was amazed at the response from the neighborhood and her tight group of friends, she is no stranger to lending a hand. For the past three years, she had staged an event at the boutique called "Hearts and Handbags," which involved middle school and older elementary girls recommended by their local schools. On a day close to Valentine's Day, Alta would hold a workshop to teach the teens confidence and self-compassion, emphasizing that each of these young women are worthy of all the possibilities that life has to offer. Not only did the girls participate in empowerment lessons and exercises, but they also received handbags filled with goodies donated by Alta's friends and colleagues. Each year the event has grown in the numbers of providers and attendees, and it is a reflection of the Altatude mission and vision.

Alta has had a year of joy as well as loss. She remains optimistic and credits her belief in God, as well as prayer, meditation and the power of community to see her through and back into business once again.

As of this writing, Alta is awaiting her landlord's renovations and insurance settlements, but she has begun to market and sell through e-commerce. She continues to be optimistic about the future. "We women are resilient and innovative, and as my grandma taught me, dream big and push through the fears," she says.

Elizabeth
HARK BECKER

Splendid Gardens

Elizabeth Hark Becker is a hands-on entrepreneur, literally as well as figuratively. In the male-dominated industry of the landscape profession, she has carved out a very successful niche by following her instincts as well as using her skills. Although she has a capable right-hand man and an excellent staff with years of experience, her fingerprints are all over every design and every landscape installation produced by her company. And to her, this is one of the two keys to the success of her business. The other is her people.

In any small business where there is a sole owner, that person has a significant impact on, as well as total responsibility for, every aspect of the company. Often, in the beginning, the founder "does it all," from operations to strategic planning to implementation to taking out the trash. Those who have been there know it all too well. Setting a mission and goals, managing finances and maximizing profitability frequently take a back seat to just getting the work done and maintaining enough staff to do it. Elizabeth knew from day one that customer and employee care were going to be key to her success. She maintains that view today.

Elizabeth began her professional career in Dallas, Texas, as an account executive for a shipping company, followed by her role as a senior account executive with another firm handling logistics for national

SHE *Elizabeth*

import accounts. Her expertise in dealing with personalities, cultures, schedules and problem-solving, as well as product lines and importing concerns, gave Elizabeth a depth of knowledge that could be carried into any field. She was keenly aware of the importance of relationships, whether within the corporate structure or in dealing with customers, both domestic and international. Although she learned a lot in these roles, her innate ability to empathize and understand business dealings from the customer's point of view put her in a unique position to succeed at business development. She pivoted to grow even more within sales roles in the landscape industry. She was recruited to work in sales for a prestigious landscape company, primarily to increase sales in additional markets. As she succeeded in this new industry, she was sought out by larger companies to work the same magic for them. After increasing her knowledge in operations and business development during successful stints at three landscape companies, Elizabeth was ready to strike out on her own.

Splendid Gardens opened its doors in 2007, with Elizabeth Hark Becker and a friend heading up full operations. Initially the firm offered a residential design/build/maintain model, which remains the core of the business offerings today. After the colleague left the company, Elizabeth took over full responsibility for customers, staffing and operations. Business researchers indicate that finances, marketing/sales and products are the magic three ingredients of new startups. Elizabeth has never wavered from focusing on her customer relationships and care for her employees. She knows that a marketing budget does not have to be large in order to grow a business. She values referrals and word-of-mouth advertising to grow her sales. Experts in the green industry agree that customer referrals are one of the best sources to grow any company. Referrals close at a higher rate than any other marketing channels, and the customers are easier to retain. Elizabeth knew this, and with the residential market as her focus, it was even more important to follow all the golden rules of customer care. Be on time, be in budget, do what you say you are going to do and deliver beyond the customers' expectations. These are the guidelines of Elizabeth's business model.

Leveraging customer care, especially if it is a natural talent of a small-business owner, can help small businesses succeed over the large regional or national companies. Truly satisfied customers have no reason to look elsewhere … and they tell their friends. Some of Elizabeth's basic rules are honesty and integrity (own up to goofs because they happen), exceeding expectations (underpromise and overdeliver), being true to the vision (stick to what you do well without chasing rainbows) and treating employees the way you wish them to treat the clients.

Projects with Splendid Gardens often involve extensive conversations between clients and designers to obtain information and uncover dreams and desires for either a new residential landscape or an updated facelift. Utilizing innate skills of listening and empathy, Elizabeth is able to establish a rapport that extends beyond just delivering a perfect landscape. A relationship has been established.

Fostering a family atmosphere amongst her staff also comes naturally for Elizabeth. They all work together to produce an exquisite outcome for each client. This comes in the form of residential site beautifications or seasonal/holiday displays, which are very popular in the neighborhoods where Splendid Gardens works. Elizabeth and her staff work closely in sync to interpret customers' visions in order to complete all enhancements in a timely manner, whether it's a bounty of spring or fall color, or seasonal décor during December. And to make all this happen in a way that creates raving customers, Elizabeth and her staff must be fully

coordinated and aligned. Every crew member understands that they must work in harmony and unison to get the job done and delivered. And the eagerness to produce is apparent. Elizabeth shows appreciation and care toward every member of her staff. They know they are appreciated and understand that they reflect the values of the company. Acts of respect and kindness are a way of life within Splendid Gardens. She injects her enthusiasm and care into every task and every staff member. Even though results are evident in the success of the organization, it is Elizabeth who is a success. She is intelligent, hard-working, ethical and intentional in being in relationship with the people on her team and those she serves.

Nicole
BUERGERS

Bee2Bee Honey Collective

Nicole Buergers characterizes herself as a woman who has always had odd or unusual jobs. She calls herself the "queen of the side hustle." While some may consider this moniker to mean that she has casually approached various means of employment, it is anything but. Although she has had multiple means of earning income, she has always been focused and intensely serious about the success of whatever position she has held. According to the Bureau of Labor statistics, the average person has 12 jobs during the span of 32 years. The number is higher if the individual has a longer work life. Career tracks are often changed during a person's professional life—seven times on average. Each change brings new information and new experiences to an individual. Learned talents provide a richness of character and abilities for the next step of a career path. Changes might be considered course correction rather than errors in fulfilling a life purpose.

As the first of five siblings to attend college, Nicole approached her studies with determination and passion. After graduating with a degree from the University of Texas at Arlington, she traveled to France to study French before returning to Atlanta with a friend to work in customer service. Her drive and talents were appreciated by the business owner, who subsequently asked her to expand her duties to internet marketing, where she created and managed an online marketing campaign for the company's brand.

Nicole continued to hone her skills in internet marketing and accepted positions in Corpus Christi then Houston. As marketing manager for an internet marketing firm, she played an integral role in marketing and branding through the website and social media. She was also considered the search engine optimization specialist for the firm and led efforts to increase the online presence for various companies in the marketplace.

Living in Houston, Nicole discovered an upscale cheese shop that specialized in the curation of artisanal American cheeses. They sought out the best of handmade cheeses and provided them to the Houston market. Nicole was a lover of all things cheese and began to work with them on a part-time basis, becoming knowledgeable in every facet of their cheese operation.

As her interest in cheese and working in specialty foods increased, burnout in the internet marketing profession set in, and Nicole made the decision to pursue her interests in the food industry. Knowing her talent and value to the agency, she was offered a promotion in order to encourage her to stay with the firm, but the nudge to move on was strong. During the same period, she happened to watch a documentary on bees. She became fascinated with them, not only as an insect population, but also their history, their culture and their ability to produce a valuable food source for consumption by humans. She took classes in home beekeeping and became hooked. She joined a local hobbyist group and started keeping her own hives, went to conferences and gradually became proficient in urban beekeeping. She soaked up every bit of

information, whether from educational sources or other hobbyists in the area. She was consumed with all things "bee."

Realizing that she was not satisfied working in the internet marketing arena, her partner encouraged her to follow her passion and create a business in Houston which filled the need for education as well as mentorship in the home beekeeping industry. Understanding how challenging it had been for her to learn and establish hives on her own, she wanted to create a business that focused on urban beekeeping. She sought to provide all of the materials and installations of hives for homeowners, as well as to mentor them through the often-difficult process in establishing successful honey-producing hives.

Until Nicole established Bee2Bee Honey Collective in 2016, those interested in setting up hives in their city environment had difficulty finding information or follow-up assistance. In addition, they had little or no way to market the product (honey) that the bees produced. Nicole's business model included delivery and setup of hives, mentorship and assistance in keeping the hives "humming" smoothly and education in how to maintain them throughout the year. Through her "Be a Keeper" program, she assists with the setup of a bee hive, installs the bees, gives instruction on how to maintain the hive, and follows up with regular checkups through the first year and honey harvest. The mentorship program is continued until the owner is comfortable enough to take care of the bees alone. Because bees often produce more honey than a homeowner can use, Nicole will also accept 35% of her clients' honey

harvest and sell for them, either through her own internet marketing or the cheese shop where she has worked.

One important lesson Nicole has learned is to ask for advice and assistance. The gentle nudge by her partner to leave a job that didn't satisfy her and to pursue her passion was a blessing. Although she did not feel that her business was initially well capitalized, she was able to raise a significant amount through crowdfunding to get her started and on her way. She was also surprised at the number of individuals who provided expertise and advice in setting up her business.

When it comes to internet marketing and online education, Nicole has bundles of knowledge and experience. While she continues to sell products through the cheese shop, specialty shops, restaurants and farmers markets, she sells a significant amount through online sales. Online classes are a new addition and have become quite popular. By continuing to educate and mentor, Nicole is spreading knowledge of the value of bees in our food chain and providing a mechanism for those interested in maintaining their own supply of local honey. The honey that is sold through Bee2Bee is always identified by the neighborhood where it is produced, which has become an important factor in marketing. Each harvest is symbolic of a specific place and time. Each colony has their own nectar and pollen preferences, and it comes through in the taste of the honey. The discriminating consumer of honey appreciates the difference. Because Nicole knows and appreciates the value of advice and receiving guidance, she makes this the cornerstone of her business model in order to grow the number of committed and informed apiarists (beekeepers).

Carmen
DAVAILUS

Carmen's Legacy Productions
& Doggies for Dementia

Some individuals have so much to offer the world that it is impossible to contain it all in one dimension. Carmen Davailus gives of herself to others through her profession, through her art and through a nonprofit constructed from a life of commitment to those who cannot speak for themselves. And as she says, "Love. It's why I do what I do." That covers all the bases.

Carmen started her career of love and care as a holistic family nurse practitioner. After receiving her RN degree, she worked in medicine until, as a single mom, she decided to get her M.S. degree in order to become a nurse practitioner, ultimately moving to Austin, Texas. She began her practice in elder care, working with seniors and their families in their homes and in a medical office setting. Over her 40 years in nursing, she touched the lives of thousands of people, not only as a provider of medical services but more deeply as a connection where individuals could find meaning and support when life handed them unexpected bad news.

As Carmen developed close relationships with her elder patients and their families, she began to understand the ramifications of dementia and Alzheimer's diagnoses. Although worldwide, 47.5 million families are affected by dementia, with Alzheimer's disease being the sixth-leading cause of death, the disease is not well understood. Alzheimer's is

a neurodegenerative disease, which, like other dementias, attacks the brain, robbing the individual of memories and skills. The medications currently on the market for the disease only help curb symptoms marginally, and very little money goes to research to find a cure and treatments.

Friends and family members of Alzheimer's patients can be confused and at a loss for words when confronted with a diagnosis. Conversations are uncomfortable. They don't feel like they have the right words or know how to "make it better." A serious illness could also remind them of their own mortality. Carmen's goal has been to remove the stigma attached to the disease.

As she listened to affected families tell their stories of sadness, disappointment and isolation, she came to realize that her ability to help might also be provided in other unique ways. While at home taking a personal day, she happened across a free class offered by an online classroom platform. The class was in photography. She learned how a camera can be a tool to tell stories. The proverbial lightbulb went off, and Carmen realized that the stories her families had to tell could be documented digitally. Over the next year, she planned, saved, prepared, learned and listened. She knew that leaving her profession to start a business as a creative would be scary, but she and her families had stories to tell in pictures and in words. She selected 13 families to interview and photograph, and over the following months, spent her time preparing their stories. The result was her book "Just See Me: Sacred Stories from the Other Side of Dementia," which was published in 2018 and has served as the launching pad for both of her businesses: Carmen's Legacy Productions and Doggies for Dementia.

Carmen states in her book that she wrote it "so the world could witness the incredible power of storytelling, love and legacy even in the face of tragedy." As a result of the success of her book, Carmen has traveled the world as a popular invited speaker on the topic of Alzheimer's awareness. She currently writes articles, hosts a popular podcast and continues to photograph individuals and their loved ones affected by dementia. Her mission is to include beautiful photos in order to preserve memories for families. Her website offers information and resources to provide support through unknown medical and emotional territory.

In addition to Carmen's work with families experiencing dementia, she also offers portrait and lifestyle photography, always setting a goal to make the experience enjoyable and personalize it to the wishes of the subject. Carmen's photography reflects the spirit and inner light of each individual, with settings tailored to them. She approaches her art with love, creativity and kindness, which are apparent when subjects see their final photos.

Carmen's Legacy Productions has grown a large customer base with numerous repeat customers, all through word of mouth and social media. Now that Carmen has mastered the skills of internet marketing, she provides graphics and assists others in making the most of their own social media through her photography.

After three years of photographing families for her book, Carmen established the Doggies for Dementia Foundation in 2018 as a 501(c)(3)
organization. Doggies is a nonprofit corporation which utilizes a family's
pets to bring about public awareness and raise funds to support those
impacted by Alzheimer's disease and dementia. After her book was
launched, she began to hear from those who had lost family members
telling her that they regretted not having family portrait sessions done.
Carmen knew she had an opportunity to correct this, and Doggies for
Dementia was born. Why are four-legged friends the ambassadors of

awareness? Carmen noticed that the images of families most appreciated by the subjects, as well as by viewers, were the ones with family pets. Carmen's family sessions do not require that a dog be present in them, but they often are included. Carmen's two four-legged family members, Sparky and Yoshi, serve to promote awareness (mostly Sparky, the chief canine officer). This is accomplished through Carmen's photography, through her writing and public speaking and through providing a platform for others to share their personal experiences.

Sparky often appears in social media messages because he assists Carmen with many of her writing and speaking tasks. Carmen, her board, her numerous advisors and her pups work consistently to spread the message, dispel myths and ease anxiety about dementia. Her mission is to provide a platform for education and awareness. Her purpose is to do it from a place of compassion and love.

Nelly
GARCIA

Rocheli Patisserie

Nelly Garcia is one of the many success stories of business startups in Austin, Texas. She was a 15-year-old young woman who immigrated to Austin from Monterrey, Mexico, and became the owner of a thriving French baking business. Nelly has made business magic happen through dedication, hard work, a commitment to learning and, above all, by sharing what she has learned and empowering the next generation to follow in her footsteps.

Latinx individuals are taking the lead in small business startups, according to a report from the Congressional Joint Economic Committee. "The rate of new entrepreneurs has recently been much higher for Latinx than for any other group—1.7 times more likely to start businesses. Latina-owned businesses have a higher growth rate (10%) than Latino businesses (6%)." Nelly is doing her part to encourage and mentor those who want emulate her path.

Nelly credits her mother, who is a chef, for influencing her early career choices. After working in several restaurants as a waitress and cook and completing a cake decorating class in high school, Nelly casually suggested to her mom that they enroll in a cake decorating class in order to do a creative activity together. Although her sister took Nelly's spot in the class, the three family members began to work together initially and somewhat

SHE *Nelly*

casually in what Nelly calls their "side hustle." Nelly was busy with school, attending Brigham Young University and working in the hospitality industry. The pastry trio continued learning all they could about the fine art of cakes and other confections by attending workshops and seminars and watching instructional YouTube videos. Their early clients were family and friends who enjoyed the benefits of having three talented women creating for all occasions.

From 2012-2013, the learning and development continued. As part of a workshop in 2013, Nelly earned the trio the opportunity to work in Las Vegas alongside Buddy Valastro from TLC television's reality blockbuster show "Cake Boss." He was so impressed with the Garcia

trio that they have been invited back three times, honing their skills with each opportunity. Back in Austin, the baking and business planning continued. In 2013, after creating a business plan for the dream business, Rocheli Patisserie, Nelly was recognized as the top college entrepreneur in a rigorous national competition put on by Entrepreneur magazine. This was just the beginning of numerous honors as Nelly completed her education and positioned her future business for success. In the same year, she was honored by Austin Monthly Magazine as a Game Changer who was transforming the world in the Under 30 category. This was

followed by her inclusion in a Forbes magazine celebration issue of brilliant businesswomen in the 30 Under 30 category. And then it happened. Nelly graduated with a degree in international business, and it was time to move Rocheli Patisserie from part-time status to full-blown endeavor.

They launched the business in 2016. Rocheli specializes in novelty cakes, which are not only beautiful but delicious. Novelty cakes include a wide range of styles with elements unlike more traditional/standard cakes. They may be traditional in shape but then are decorated in themes or unusual/atypical styles. Sometimes the cake fools the mind into thinking it is an object rather than a cake. It was important from the beginning that the creations be jaw-dropping from first peek and then delight when eaten. The highest quality ingredients and taste are as important to the Rocheli team as the visual beauty of each creation. Frequently, novelty cakes appear as works of art but taste is left in the mixing bowl—but not by Rocheli Patisserie. The Garcia family has also branched out into cookies and fancy pastries, which they create for holidays, traditional occasions and any other event or festivity the brain can conceive.

Although the creation of the cakes and pastries was initially in the Garcia kitchen, at the end of 2016, Nelly rented a commercial kitchen in order to expand. They occupied this kitchen from 2016 until 2020 and have since opened their own brick-and-mortar bakery on 12th and Chicon in Austin.

How has the business grown? Although word of mouth and the beauty of the products have been the best advertising to date, social media has

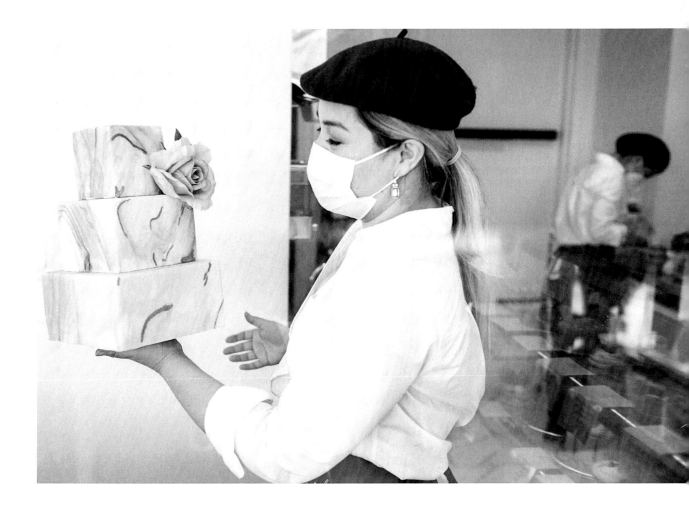

been the primary vehicle for getting the word out. When individuals receive one of the Rocheli creations, anyone who sees it will never order from another bakery.

Although Nelly and family work very hard at creating custom sweet delights, she is also keenly aware of the importance of giving back and nurturing the next generation of chefs and women business owners. In the bakery, customers will find interns working alongside Nelly, learning from someone who is invested in their future as well as her own.

SHE Nelly

Jill
GRIFFIN

Jill Griffin and Associates

As a little girl growing up in Marshville, North Carolina (population less than 3,000), Jill Griffin was already pondering big ideas. Sitting attentively in her third grade class, she observed that the teacher she much admired was intelligent, likable, caring and unmarried. Jill asked herself how it was that this woman seemed so different, not just unmarried, but independent and confident and capable. And above all, her teacher was well educated. *That* was what Jill wanted to be when she grew up. Not necessarily a teacher, but educated, independent and capable. Objective No. 1 set.

During this time in her life, Jill frequently walked from her home to the town square to do the typical shopping a child does, sharing her disposable income with the local merchants on purchases that all little children buy. Observant as she was, Jill noticed that some of the locally owned mom and pop stores were more popular than others. And she wanted to know why. Objective No. 2 set.

Attending the University of South Carolina allowed Jill to be independent and investigate the fine art of targeted marketing through customer care. She graduated magna cum laude with a bachelor's and then a master's in business administration from the Moore School of Business, becoming the educated, independent and confident woman she envisioned. While

SHE *jill*

at the university studying marketing, she was able to home in on the answer to her question about why people prefer one business over another. Her curiosity and her question were her purpose. One of her early positions while in the MBA program was as advertising manager for The Daily Gamecock, the independent student newspaper, where she began to perfect her skills in becoming a resource of choice for advertisers. Her work became her passion.

Following graduation, she had her choice of several offers and settled on a position with an international firm in their brand management track. After moving up through the ranks over six years, she responded to an ad in the Wall Street Journal for the position of director of marketing and sales in the hospitality industry. This new adventure would allow her to flex her entrepreneurial muscles by organizing and overseeing a staff and by moving to Texas, which she considered a great adventure.

After two years, she believed she was ready to make her next professional moves. She would start her own business consulting firm as that independent, confident and focused woman *and* dive deeply into the research on answering her questions regarding customer loyalty. She wanted to share her findings with many others who had the same questions. And the idea for her first book was born.

SHE *gill*

While doing initial research on her book, Jill taught at the University of Texas in the business school, which provided her with fertile ground for exploring additional questions regarding the relationship between businesses and customers. In addition, as she created and wrote, she established a client base in consulting. In doing research and expanding upon her experience in marketing in corporate America, Jill deduced that customers have different loyalty needs depending on where they are in the business lifecycle. She knew that "suspects" have different needs than prospects and that first-time customers have different needs than repeat customers. Her first book, "Customer Loyalty: How to Earn It, How to Keep It," was (and is) a big success. Along with large and small business client purchases, the United States Postal Service selected the book to distribute to 22,000 small businesses to encourage them to use direct mail. In the book, Jill described every customer stage and how to fully understand them in order to ensure customer loyalty.

Over three decades, Jill has continued to lead workshops and seminars, write articles and hold the respected position as one of the country's preeminent authorities on customer loyalty. She has appeared on "Fox News" and writes regular articles on up-and-coming business authorities for Forbes.com. Jill has written two other books that specifically address customer loyalty and win-back strategies. She believes that becoming an author was an important component of her career. The knowledge that a professional has gained over the years is expanded when it is shared with others. She has never had formal mentors, although she credits many advisors for giving her help when she needed it. She also holds her third grade teacher in high regard as someone who sparked her enthusiasm for being independent, confident and "putting herself out there."

Jill is open, outgoing and has a network of friends, and for these qualities she credits her selection as a board of director member and then vice-president of an international restaurant group where she has served for almost 20 years. By serving on this corporate board, Jill came to appreciate the diversity of a board's membership and was encouraged to write a book for women seeking board membership. Since its publication, "Earn Your Seat on a Corporate Board: 7 Actions to Build Your Career, Elevate Your Leadership, and Expand Your Influence" has led to an increasing number of women holding seats on boards.

Jill has also written two books on leadership. "Women Make Great Leaders" identifies women who have answered the call to leadership, telling their personal stories of what it took to succeed as courageous and focused leaders. "Follow These Leaders" tells stories in the subjects' own words of how they achieved individual success, often with trial and error. This collection of advice from scores of successful people in Jill's life is a reflection of the questions that we would all like to ask really smart people, and Jill did just that.

In her current work life, Jill is translating her marketing expertise and customer loyalty wisdom into e-courses. Her first online course, "Unlock Customer Value for Fast, Reliable Growth," launched in 2021. As she prepares each presentation, each article, she is grateful to possess a curious mind. One never knows where the answers will lead.

Sheila
HAWKINS-BUCKLEW

Hawkins Bucklew Jewelry Designs

Sheila Hawkins-Bucklew's business, as well as fashion advice, is impeccable. She's also a person who people welcome as a friend. Her focus on achieving goals is keen and her mission is clear. She believes that entrepreneurship equals freedom, especially for women. She has sought that for herself and now provides the same opportunities for others.

Growing up in Pittsburgh, Pennsylvania, Sheila gained considerable experience in retail as a young woman. She graduated from Duquesne University in Pittsburgh with a bachelor's degree in business administration and started her professional career in retail buying and store management. A move to Austin, Texas, with her husband and daughter resulted in a period where she focused on her role as a stay-at-home mom while her daughter was young. Sheila returned to the workforce in real estate sales after taking classes and passing the test to become a licensed realtor. She found great success as a realtor because, as a die-hard achiever, nothing less would do. She was named Rookie of the Year by her first employer and Realtor of the Year and President of the Women's Council of the Austin Board of Realtors. She also served on the board of directors of the Austin Board of Realtors. In real estate, the client base typically is sourced from those you know. After the move from Pittsburgh, she knew no one, but being focused on success, Sheila

SHE Sheila

could not be stopped. At first, she worked as an agent, then as a broker leading her own firm.

Freedom through entrepreneurship was not merely a goal, it was a way of life for Sheila—in everything she mastered. In real estate, she was sought out for advice and mentorship and realized that this, too, was her calling—the calling of supporting and inspiring others to achieve their goals.

An essential part of every day for Sheila has always been prayer. Her prayers include gratitude and hope for the best for herself and her family, as well as an invitation for guidance on her purpose in life—to be the best she can be at whatever task allows her to live her highest good. After a period of time, she began to feel the nudge to pursue a creative path in her personal and professional life. She wanted to provide support and develop avenues for others to create. The answer was not what she expected. She had been all about business and had not honed her skills as a creative. But she knew that if this was how God was directing her, she would certainly listen … and learn, approaching this new venture with the passion and gusto that were her trademarks.

Hawkins Bucklew Jewelry Designs was born in October 2013. The vision for this new venture was one of authentic living with an emphasis on individual style. Not only did she set about to design and create a meaningful line of unique jewelry, but she also knew that it was

important to continue her commitment to empowering other women to gain freedom through entrepreneurship.

Sheila was quickly noticed. Her designs were included in Austin Fashion Week and received editorial mentions in magazines such as British Vogue, Tribeza magazine and The Austin Chronicle. She also launched her designs in Macy's stores. While Hawkins Bucklew Jewelry Designs was gaining a reputation, Sheila found herself mentoring women entrepreneurs during a special trip to Nigeria to facilitate the Creative Entrepreneurship Boot Camp for women. This experience fueled her resolve to create the same environment back in Austin.

As Sheila designed and produced her own line of ethos-chic statement jewelry, she also created a collaborative marketplace named Showroom 808, which provides the opportunity for local creative women to have a physical space for their designs. She knew that many women are not able to afford their own brick-and-mortar spaces as they are starting their lines. Showroom 808 was created to solve this problem, and it provides programs and services to help stimulate economic development. Through an application process which ensures that the businesses are 100% women-owned and produce original and unique designs of high quality, Sheila selects female entrepreneurs to join the collective. Hawkins Bucklew Jewelry and Showroom 808 began in a small retail space in north Austin but moved to a stylish location in The Domain just before Christmas 2020.

Sheila is aware that there are many challenges to scaling a small business. Statistics bear out that only 4.2% of women entrepreneurs grow their companies to over $1 million in sales. And for women of color, that number drops to 1%. One major challenge for women starting a business is funding. Startups seeking venture capital are often funded by companies that have investors who are similar in education, gender and ethnicity. Only 6% of VC companies have women on the board, and this makes obtaining capital difficult for women. Fortune magazine reported that in 2019, startups founded solely by women received

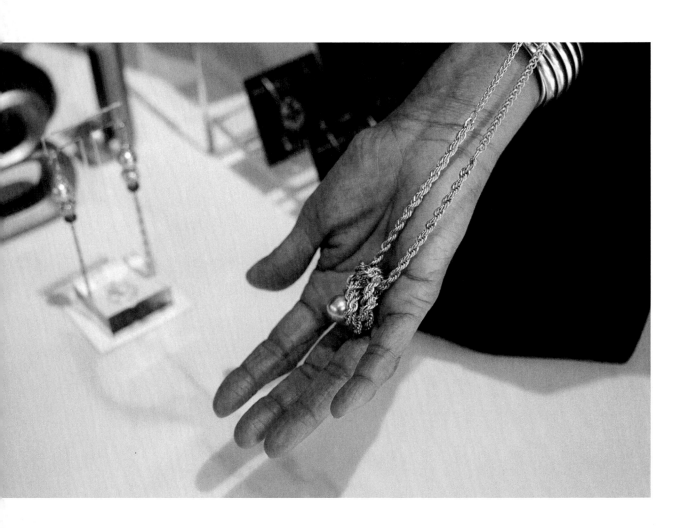

only 2.7% of the total venture capital investment in the United States. Women-driven small startups that may not seek venture capital often receive small amounts of assistance from friends or family. Sheila's goal is to help close the gap between bootstrap and venture capital support.

Sheila has received recognition for her efforts to inspire and empower women in the U.S. and abroad. She received the Mandela Washington Fellowship Exchange Award from the U.S. State Department and has been a recipient of the Profile of Prominence awarded by the National Women of Achievement. Sheila was honored by the nonprofit community television station in Austin, AFTV5, as the Entrepreneur of the Year in 2018. They also recognized her with the African Champion Award-Entrepreneur of the Year. Her recognition will continue as she helps create opportunities for others. Her most notable award? It is the one that repeats itself daily—knowing she has done her part to inspire and advance women, like herself, who desire economic and professional freedom.

Lindsey
HOHLT

Lindsey Leigh Jewelry

In the modern vernacular, "adding fuel to the fire" is often considered as making a bad thing worse. Not so in the business mindset of Lindsey Hohlt (aka Houston Diamond Girl), founder and owner of Lindsey Leigh Jewelry in Houston, Texas. Without hesitation, Lindsey will share that in her case, turning an uncomfortable working environment into an opportunity to soar came from realizing that we have choices. We can accept non-supportive work environments that hold us back from reaching our full potential, or we can let a negative situation provide the fuel to fire us up to take a chance on our own abilities and talents. This is what Lindsey chose.

As reported in Business News Daily, women in 2020 faced challenges to entrepreneurship that were not faced by men. Some of these include defying social expectations that women cannot be seen as serious business owners. When a woman walks into a room of professionals in her industry, she is often one of a handful of females, depending upon the industry. Globally, 6.2% of all women are business owners while 9.5% of all men have established businesses (where "established" is defined as longer than 42 months). This trend is changing, though. The number of women and men who intend to start a business within the next three years is approaching parity between male- and female-owned businesses. The greatest number of women-founded startups is in the 25-44 age group, a time when women are just getting into their first career or beginning to move into a second.

Defying social expectations is only one of the intangibles that seem to hold women back. It is true that finding investors is more difficult for women than for men and especially for women of color. That trend, too, is changing. Lack of mentorship is often an issue. Finding women who can offer support and assistance, especially in one's field, is daunting. Almost half (48%) of female founders report that a lack of available advisors and mentors limits their professional growth, according to Inc. Magazine. Yet, the majority of the barriers to become a business owner come from within the future entrepreneur herself.

In Lindsey's case, there were no other women gemologists/business owners with whom to network. Being an avid learner, she not only sought professional designations from the Gemological Institute of America but also asked questions and observed others in her field who happened to all be male.

Other roadblocks to starting a woman-owned business have been identified by many business sources. The communal, consensus-building qualities encouraged in young girls can leave women unintentionally downplaying their own worth. Without fully grasping the impact of her early activities, Lindsey began to build a strong sense of self early in life, and this would help to bolster her resolve to branch out on her own when the time was right.

As a high school student, six-foot-tall Lindsey began a career as a runway and print model for a Houston agency. Wearing fashionable clothing (and expensive jewelry), Lindsey was often in the spotlight as the center of attention. After high school, she attended Louisiana State University and studied fashion merchandising and business, continuing to model as opportunities arose. Her career in modeling continued until 2019. After college, Lindsey returned to Houston, where she worked in retail fashion until she was hired by a local upscale jewelry store as assistant manager. Because of her hard work, enthusiasm and willingness to do what was necessary for the shop to be successful, she was promoted to manager within six months. She handled over 60 lines of jewelry. She traveled solo to market and was tasked with buying lines that would sell well. Lindsey paid attention. She learned not only to seek out and buy jewelry, but also learned how to manage many of the ongoing business functions and staff. When an opportunity to work with a custom bridal-only group came to her, she took it, and another learning trajectory took off. Working in an appointment-only custom design business gave her a perspective on what she might do on her own one day. Working in a male-dominated industry that catered to the desires of women (custom engagement and wedding design) gave her great insight into how she would craft her business someday, when the time was right.

Working with women and their partners at the most exciting time in their lives? Yes! Providing custom engagement and wedding jewelry? Yes! And giving them special treatment at special times in their lives? Double yes! So, in May of 2018, Lindsey Leigh Jewelry was born. Working out of her husband's study, she began to spread the news that she was in business. Through friends and acquaintances and then social media, she launched herself as Houston Diamond Girl. The unique, caring service, paired with an eye for quality and detail in custom jewelry, started her business on a success trajectory, primarily through referrals. By summer she had her first custom order through her newly minted website.

By the time autumn came, Lindsey had outgrown the small startup space and moved into a retail location in order to fulfill the growing number of custom orders, although the majority of her business was still by appointment only and custom designed. Two years in the rented space, and it was time to grow again. As more floor space was added, Lindsey realized she needed staff to assist. Handling every aspect of a growing business, which requires close customer care, impeccable design plus all of the business organization tactics, needs more than two hands to handle. Letting go of a highly personal business was not easy. Until the fall of 2020, all communication was handled with one cellphone line—Lindsey's. This, too, had to change.

2020 was the year of moving into Lindsey Leigh Jewelry's own building and expanding. With the onset of the city business closures due to the pandemic, Lindsey followed suit and closed for six weeks. What was most surprising was the increase in online shopping due to people being sequestered at home. Jewelry sales increased, and Lindsey and her staff stayed busy.

As a self-proclaimed optimist, Lindsey knows there is a bright future for herself, her family (she gave birth to a baby boy in December 2020) and her business and growing staff. She plans to grow the business, spend quality time with her family, provide unique and personalized wedding jewelry and travel the world. This confident and extremely talented woman is the one who can make it happen. She has embraced the fuel that feeds her fire.

Sandra
HUTCHENS

AND *Jamie*
KLINGENBERG

Gardens for Texas

Sandra Hutchens and Jamie Klingenberg are business partners … and still friends after 17-plus years in business together. Partnerships are challenging, whether they are formed on the basis of love, friendship, interests or with money in mind. We know that 70% of partnerships in the U.S. end in split-ups, with some of them being on the south side of nasty. Arguments over finances (often the basis for business relationships) are high on the list of issues that break down a partnership. At the core of the business failure is often a lack of planning at the beginning, as well as a lack of common values and vision. In the beginning of a collaboration, the mood is often excitement and enthusiasm at working on common interests. The drudgery of asking questions about the long term isn't the fun part. Doing the work and getting the business off the ground has all the sparkle. Sandra and Jamie have worked hard to start right and stay focused, and they are making their partnership work.

In the beginning, the common link between these two talented women was that they were neighbors in Dallas, Texas. Sandra had completed her Master of Business Administration degree and was working in marketing, while Jamie was on staff at a local garden center and nursery. Ideas come in all forms and when least expected, and the notion to start a landscape business revealed itself during Sandra's prayer practice. When she approached Jamie with the idea, the business was born.

SHE Sandra

Sandra used many of the concepts she had learned in business school to build a business plan (with Jamie) as they launched Gardens for Texas. Communication about their individual visions for the company helped them craft their plans to start and to grow. Both of these ladies are excellent communicators, which, from the beginning, helped them create relationships. It has been one of the sources of success as they acquired and retained a solid customer base. Sandra believes Jamie to be the perfect partner because she is motivated, dedicated and inspiring to her and their staff. Likewise, Jamie appreciates Sandra's kindness and empathy toward their crews, even though Sandra is a stickler for abiding by all of the guidelines—written and unwritten—that they have set.

For both of these equal partners in Gardens of Texas, time has flown by since that first meeting. They have made no major changes to their original business plan and are quite happy with the structure and size of the business. It is manageable for the partners and gives them the personal rewards and flexibility that they initially sought.

Gardens of Texas is a residential landscape firm that offers original designs from the ground up. Through extensive interviews and collaboration with homeowners, using years of experience as well as intuition, both women produce creative solutions to problems in the landscape. Their innovation results in traditional, formal, casual or (their favorite) xeriscape gardens, which delight the homeowners. The design process requires a lot of communication, which is natural for them both. Once a design is complete, installation begins. This may include irrigation, hardscapes and structures, a variety of adapted plant material, seasonal color, container gardens and vegetable gardens. The results are not only beautiful but functional and completely unique for each homeowner.

One measure of success for any business is repeat business. Through the hard work at customizing all landscape plans and installations, and through careful listening and follow-up, Gardens of Texas has many repeat customers. Whether they are hired to do small touch-ups or renovations or start from scratch at new homes, their client base thinks of them first when planning new landscape work. One of their clients told them that the newly executed landscape at their home "changed their lives," which is music to the ears of the two creative partners. Sandra and Jamie's intuitive design work, coupled with attention to their clients' wishes, keeps their customers coming back.

Both women are aware that their business comes from referrals as well as repeat customers. They have done no advertising, although they do make sure to address search engine optimization so that their company is "top of mind" when individuals seek out high-end residential landscape work or xeriscape design experts. They also keep their website up to date with educational information for existing and potential clients and have an extensive gallery of photos that highlight their design expertise, along with before and after images. They know the saying "A picture is worth a thousand words" is true and make sure the images are top quality, showing off the best of their projects.

The business partners have never subscribed to the advice of Lou Holtz, former football player, coach and analyst who stated, "In this world you're either growing or you're dying so get in motion and grow." These partners believe that success is defined differently for them than just profit and loss statements. Yes, it's essential to make sure the company is financially solid so they can deliver quality products and services and care for all team members. They have found that happiness is so much more than sales growing year over year. They agree that identifying their talents and gifts and delivering results that make clients happy is their focus. For the two of them, personal success is defined not by money, but by quality of life and feeling fulfilled. Research has shown that having strong connections and access to nature make individuals happiest. The Gardens for Texas relationship is fortunate to have both. The robust partnership of these two women, plus the opportunity to provide goods and services in nature, have given them the maximum opportunity for happiness. As business partners and friends, they spend their days beautifying the world for others, 17 years and counting!

LaToncia (Dee)
JONES

Coffee Truck Owner

Dee Jones knows that starting a business isn't for the faint of heart. The experience of bringing into being a new entity that has never before existed, and watching it grow and take shape and fulfill dreams, is something that cannot be duplicated. As the Wide World of Sports used to announce, "the thrill of victory and the agony of defeat," is all incorporated in the launching and operation of one's own business. But as Dee's son and biggest supporter describes his mom, "She is driven."

Dee grew up in Detroit, Michigan, and at an early age went to work for the United States Postal Service. As a single mom, it was essential that she be able to provide for herself and her son. She accomplished that in short order but knew that someday there would be more. She had a sincere desire to own her own business and knew that, for the time being, patience was her best friend. As she gained experience and tenure with the postal service, she asked for a transfer and relocated to Austin, Texas, where she and her son settled in the suburb of Manor. She continued to dream and then she began to plan for her future business.

For some people, dreaming up an idea for a new business isn't easy. The decision to build a business starts with an awareness of a need and then uncovering a solution to the problem. Living in Manor, Dee noticed the lack (and need) of a coffee shop in the central business district.

SHE *LaToncia (Dee)*

Coffee is the most popular beverage in the world, with more than 400 billion cups knocked back yearly. In the U.S. alone, more than 450 million cups of coffee are consumed every day. About half of the people in the United States over the age of 18 (107 million) drink coffee every day, which is a lot of java. And Dee observed that none of the 450 million cups are being prepared and sold in Manor, Texas. She noticed, and her business idea was born. She knew that a brick-and-mortar coffee shop was initially out of the question because of the capital required; however, a food/coffee truck was the perfect affordable option. Also, in this way, she knew she could move the business to where the action was in the form of events, expos, festivals and other outdoor happenings.

Food and beverage trucks are excellent first commercial business investments. Although there is an investment in the vehicle itself, the trucks tend to hold their value and provide the perfect first chance at starting the business. Food/beverage trucks are less risky than brick-and-mortar restaurants, they can locate and then relocate, the overhead is low and they provide new entrepreneurs with unlimited flexibility. On the flip side, vehicles for food prep are in high demand and not always easy to find. Food trucks require long hours of hard work, as does any food or beverage business. Dee is well aware of this and is ready to make it happen when the timing is right for her. She knows that once the business is up and running, statistics show that a good living is possible.

Another bonus for Dee is that her son, Emmanuel, will be an important part of her new business. She will continue to work with the postal service in the early days of the business, and he will take up the slack for her. She is no stranger to hard work. Along with being employed full time at the post office, she has also used her side hustle as a hair stylist to supplement her income. As a licensed beautician, she has always worked in a salon or on her own in addition to her day-to-day employment.

Dee has been preparing for her new venture for over a year, researching food trucks in general and coffee businesses specifically. She has devoted hours to reading and watching online training videos that provide step-by-step instructions on how to get a business focused on coffee up and succeeding. YouTube videos provide hours of information and support for new entrepreneurs looking for advice. Video content is becoming vastly more popular than written information when it comes to learning anything, but specifically for providing business advice. From TED Talks to individual "how-to" videos on startups, it is possible to learn whatever you need to get a new enterprise off and running. Dee has learned everything she needs to know about starting her coffee truck and has completed her business plan.

One of Dee's primary support systems has been her friends, specifically her good friend Yolanda who has encouraged her from the idea stage of her business plan. Self-motivation and self-discipline are essential attributes of a new entrepreneur; however, a strong support system is critical. A squad of cheerleaders from family and friends is indispensable. Dee's No. 1 fans are her son and her best friend. They have been there with her and will continue to provide physical help and emotional support. Not a day goes by that Dee and Yolanda don't talk.

Dotting all the i's and crossing all the t's, Dee will soon be ready to launch. The vision is defined, the mission is clear, her objectives are set and all of the basic strategies for startup are outlined. Her business plan has become an action plan, and her launch date is a well-kept secret for now. This driven woman has been patiently waiting for the right time.

Allegra
KAOUGH

The Naked Dog

Allegra Kaough is fluent in three languages: English, Equine and Canine. She learned English from birth and Equine as a practitioner of Natural Horsemanship in her early years. Her trajectory toward becoming an eloquent speaker of Canine occurred unintentionally but naturally. Not having dogs as pets while growing up, a path toward dog training was never part of her professional plan. As is the case with many accidental entrepreneurs, seemingly unrelated events knit together at just the right moment in life to set her on the path for which she was intended. Author Elizabeth Gilbert writes, "The universe buries strange jewels deep within us all, and then stands back to see if we can find them." Allegra Kaough is the keeper of some incredible jewels, which can result in the satisfying bonding of a pet (specifically a dog) and pet parents. She speaks fluent Dog and wants to teach it to all who are willing to learn.

By chance, Allegra temporarily lived with a dog trainer and six dogs in 2008 in Arizona while between jobs. She had never owned a dog and hadn't even been around them very much. She discovered that helping the trainer with walking duties was very therapeutic for her. Being in the out-of-doors and connecting in a one-to-one "conversation" with each of the dogs became very healing. As she slowly developed an understanding of how the dogs responded to her and she to them, she realized the importance of communicating to be understood. Professional dog

SHE *Allegra*

training was not on her radar as a business; however, she did believe she was ready for dog ownership. While in Arizona, Allegra found Harley (an adorable harlequin dachshund rescue), then packed her bags and moved to her home state, New York. Allegra apprenticed with a New York City-based dog trainer who utilized a style of training emphasizing positive reinforcement to teach tricks and simple behaviors. Although behavior may be modified after hundreds of repetitions of tricks/treats, this style does not address innate dog psychology. The problem with all-positive training is that there may come a time when the distractions that the dog faces are more interesting to the dog than the treat that the pet parent is presenting. Milk Bones don't outweigh a dog's desire to be a dog. Communication on the dog's platform of understanding has not been achieved. While apprenticing in New York City, Allegra became more convinced that trainers must not only learn to speak Dog, but pet parents must do the same. Too often, she found that pet owners would engage the services of the expert trainer with the hopes that their dog would become well trained and then they would completely undo all of the work when the pup returned home. Allegra again realized there might be a better way to lead to well-behaved, calm dogs. But to do this, the communication must be on the level of the pet.

Allegra and Harley soon relocated to Austin, Texas, and began to enjoy the countless hiking trails available for humans and their pets. During this time, Allegra began to notice a "regular" on the trail with a pack of dogs, none of whom were on leash. She observed that they were well behaved and easily obeyed the directions of the pack leader/trainer. Over time,

SHE *Allegra*

Allegra got to know the trainer and began to work on honing her own skills and building a language which made sense, not only to the trainer or pet parent, but most importantly, to the dog. Within a year, Allegra was ready to go out on her own, and she launched The Naked Dog.

Allegra likes to say that she is the trainer of humans on the subject of dogs and dog language. Armed with an understanding of the psychology of dogs in general and an owner's dog specifically, Allegra is able to bring about harmony within an individual pet and pet family. Her style is called Balance Training, one of the nine styles of dog training used by various dog trainers. Balance Training is primarily based on the psychology of dogs and their interaction with their environment. Allegra knows that the bulk of her training is to educate the pet owners to interact with their dog in a way that causes dog behavior to be respectful. The dogs come to understand that when they exhibit a particular behavior that elicits a negative response from the owner, they quickly know that in order to avoid this owner's response, they need to adjust their own actions. The results come very quickly. Owners are amazed at the polite (not submissive) behavior their pets learn. And as long as the owners continue to consistently ask for respectful dog responses, they will get them.

The training component of the business was the easy part. Testimonials and referrals brought new clients in large numbers. Pets are very important to people, and Austin has the third-highest rate of pet ownership in the nation. Finding clients has never been an issue, and there has never

been a need to advertise. Like most new entrepreneurs, Allegra felt that she was initially lacking in business expertise. In a highly communicative business environment, it became necessary fairly quickly to upgrade software to be able to handle all of the scheduling, interactions and education. The Naked Dog website offers numerous blog posts on all subjects, helping owners navigate the care and training of their new pet. Also offered are e-courses and scheduling for seminars, off-leash training, private training sessions and boarding with training options. In the early days, Allegra and her staff offered leash pack hikes daily; however, they discontinued this in 2020 and now offer off-leash training individually. Particularly popular are the puppy seminars and training, which get new owners started off on the right "paw."

In an era where our relationship with our pet is essential to our emotional well-being, it just makes sense to have a strong partnership with a dog. And as the woman who speaks Canine fluently says, "Incredible things become possible."

Melissa

LADD

Melissa Ladd LLC

Melissa Ladd is a woman you want to include in your circle of friends. First and foremost, she is deeply grounded, although she considers herself a "bit of a gypsy." She exudes health and wisdom, creativity and intelligence. Her left brain met her right brain years ago, and the result is an awesome real estate and development whiz kid as well as a delightful yoga instructor with a solid following. Melissa is a laid-back entrepreneur.

Many entrepreneurs may say that starting a business is something they always felt destined to do. Yet there are an amazing number of "accidental" entrepreneurs like Melissa—people who never in a million years thought they'd be running their own business. Also like Melissa, many do not even consider themselves entrepreneurs. Melissa has always simply done what she wanted to do in her work life and structured it exactly as she wanted in her own unique and creative manner. Independence and freedom are always two big reasons women indicate they wish to start their own businesses. Entrepreneurs want freedom for their own time and interests, freedom to spend flexible time with family and the ability to create and innovate in a way they might not find in a "normal" work world. In past generations, there were few parental role models who showed the way to ownership. With no idea of how to start or run a business, individuals moved through education and the workforce

SHE *Melissa*

believing that business ownership wasn't within their reach. But circumstances change, and we are often either propelled or dropped into the opportunities to start a business. Intentional or accidental, gypsy or set in place, no two roads to entrepreneurship are the same.

Melissa studied art in college (right brain leads the way) but left to accept a position as a bank officer (left brain kicks in) with her brother, who founded a bank in Colorado. She discovered she loved numbers, accounting and working with finances. Subsequently, she worked in the entertainment industry in the corporate office, handling operations and numbers. Still looking to handle the numbers of others, she moved to Austin, Texas, where she worked with small businesses and an art gallery, merging her left- and right-brain talents.

Along the way, Melissa exercised her creative muscle. During her formative years, she was inspired by her artist mother, and during college while on her own, she studied painting, drawing, printmaking and photography. She published her ethereal photographs of a woman in a vintage bridal gown in a book titled "Trainride." The photos in this book were shot between 1995-2008 and have been shown in galleries in New Mexico and Texas. Additionally, she aided in the creation of two short films. All the while, Melissa maintained a solid base of accounting clients in Austin.

Being an enthusiastic, energetic and curious being, Melissa made the decision to obtain her realtor's license in order to stretch her professional wings. During this time, she became captivated with the old buildings in downtown Elgin, Texas. Finding a lovely vacant and crumbling pharmacy building built in 1895, she took on the left-brain/right-brain challenge of purchasing, developing, renovating and managing it. Not only the vintage charm of the building, but the opportunity to save a historic structure motivated Melissa to take on the additional task of managing a large renovation project. She met many strong and creative women who lived in Elgin, and she appreciated the example they set for living and doing business in this small suburb of Austin.

Through unique zoning by the city of Elgin, the 2,200-square-foot building is divided into 50% commercial and 50% residential space, which allows any owner to develop the building in two separate zoning genres. Melissa was able to develop a space suitable for living and working. Through mountains of decisions about demolition and construction, Melissa guided an army of contractors through the remodel, which she considered a very creative brain process. In 2017, her project, called 28N, was complete. During the first year, the commercial space was used or leased for art shows and community events, with a few community yoga sessions sprinkled in. Eventually, Body & Shine Wellness became a permanent tenant as Melissa took on the role of landlord in addition to building owner and resident in the rear apartment. With a permanent yoga studio in residence, it was only natural that Melissa earn her yoga teacher's certificate and begin to offer regular yoga classes. During a period in 2020, Melissa taught classes on Zoom, managing the space and operating her accounting practice. Left brain continued to be in collaboration with right brain.

Melissa

Traditionally, the majority of entrepreneurs have been logical thinkers, problem-solvers and people who pay attention to details. Melissa is an excellent example of a details person; however, she does not fit the mold of a stereotypical left-brain operator. There seems to be a shift from predominantly logic-focused business owners to those who draw from visualization, creativity, relationships and collaboration, which are more in the domain of right-brainers. It is essential that those who are predominantly analytical thinkers either take up practices which help develop their creative thinking or select partners or colleagues who have these characteristics. Both creativity and analytical thinking are key to building a business that can provide the opportunities the founder seeks.

Although Melissa considers herself a "bit of a gypsy," she is also the epitome of a Renaissance woman. She can create world-class art, navigate complex financial statements, teach yoga and manage construction projects as only a proper left-brain/right-brain entrepreneur can do.

Pam

LEBLANC

Pam LeBlanc Adventures

Pam LeBlanc loved her job as a staff writer for the Austin American-Statesman, a central Texas daily newspaper. She especially loved the people. After 21 years and hundreds of adventure notches on her belt, she sought greener pastures and wider trails, as the newspaper was in staff-reduction mode and stress escalated. Pam has always been a girl with a passion for out-of-doors action, and she was eager to make that a full-time commitment.

Two decades ago, armed with a degree in agricultural journalism from Texas A&M University, Pam went to work for small Texas newspapers in Plano, then McAllen, before landing in Austin to work for the Austin American-Statesman. Initially she covered schools and general assignments before moving out-of-doors, literally. Her writing, which focused on Austin's outdoor scene, came to include a fitness column (Fit City) on a trial basis and then as a regular column for over 15 years. Pam began to flex her adventure muscles while writing for the Statesman and penned stories on her infamous participation in a naked 5K as well as a vivid description of her rappelling down a 38-story building. More sedate adventures included trekking the John Muir Trail in California and navigating the rivers of West Texas and the waters around Fiji and the Galapagos Islands. Now that she has launched Pam LeBlanc Adventures, travel and out-of-doors outrageous activities are still the sweet spots for

SHE *Pam*

Pam—a freelance writer in search of out-of-the-ordinary thrills in Texas and beyond.

At last count, there were over 57 million freelancers in all professions in the United States. These courageous individuals account for 36% of the workforce. By 2027, it is estimated that freelancers will make up the majority of the total. A lot of freelancers are millennials, with 47% of their age group heading in this direction. As 2020 unfolded and many individuals began to work from home, freelancing became an attractive alternative. Yet most freelancers work in this mode by choice rather than necessity. Flexibility, independence, the freedom to set work hours and pace, plus the opportunity to grow the business at any desired rate are attractive. Although the reported numbers are for full-time freelancers, many women are choosing to start their businesses as a side hustle prior to leaving the security of a full-time job working for others. Freelancing offers the opportunity to work on a flexible schedule. Unpredictability of clientele, opportunities and income are some of the scary parts of freelancing; however, Pam, who thrives on adventure, never looked back.

Working from home allows Pam to make her own rules and participate in a huge number of physical activities to her heart's content.

Pam's personal workout schedule is somewhat weather-dependent, but typically, she water skis on Monday mornings and swims the other weekday mornings with a master's swim group. Her transportation for most local outings is her bicycle. She rides distances that would send most of us to bed for a nap for the rest of the day. Her goal is not only to seek out and try some of the most interesting adventures you've never heard of (camel trekking, anyone?) but also to keep her readers informed and entertained. Pam has all of the wisdom of an adult and the sense of discovery and delight of a youngster. No trip, no activity, ever falls outside of what Pam might attempt and then document for readers of various magazines. And she doesn't care if she screws it up, because she gave it a try. One of her favorite sayings is, "I'm no stranger to public humiliation." And the good news is that we all get to go along for the ride.

Pam authors a blog and writes for publications of all sizes. Her articles have been in 10 major publications, including Texas Monthly, Texas Highways, Austin, Austin Fit, Texas Parks & Wildlife, Tribeza, The Alcalde and Real Simple. And she continues to contribute to the Austin American-Statesman. She's also been interviewed on many podcasts, such as "I Could Never Do That." She has backpacked over 500 miles and swam more than 7,500 miles. She is constantly on the lookout for undiscovered ramblings and adventures and is kept informed of all new things unusual by friends and fans. If asked, "Have you ever …?" and she hasn't, be assured she will.

Pam does what she does (and loves) full time now. It is possible to have a thriving professional life as well as an adventurous soul. REI conducted a nationwide survey and found that seven out of 10 women wish they could spend more time outdoors, and one of the barriers they cited was a lack of time. People often say, "I wish I had time to do that." The reality

is, it's not about having time, but making time. It is possible to work a 40-hour work week and spend time on weekends or on vacations trying some of the adventures that Pam writes about. The biggest barrier to women not following their dream of outdoor adventures is that they don't believe it is possible. Pam can tell you differently. In 2021, she and two good friends launched Austin Travels Magazine to help whet the whistle of the travel- and adventure-deprived. It includes family travel, adventure travel and day trips in Texas and beyond.

Along with her adventures and writing about them for publications, Pam authored a book titled "My Stories, All True: J. David Bamberger on Life as an Entrepreneur and Conservationist." This book communicates an endearing story of Pam's long friendship with Bamberger, who became the owner and conservator extraordinaire of a ranch called Selah in Central Texas. Over the years of their friendship, the former vacuum cleaner salesman and fried chicken luminary shared stories (mostly true) with Pam, which she has carefully gathered and shared in a down-to-earth manner.

Pam has been a writer for decades, but with her engines fueled and her sleeping bag always packed, she is ready to hit the road to add a few more of those adventure notches to her belt. And, of course, she will let us know all about them.

Susan

MALCIK

Susan Malcik ATX

Susan Malcik is, in every sense of the words, a woman of the world. Her travels and adventures, as well as global shopping, are experiences to be envied. Thirty-five years in a dozen countries has allowed her to live her dream of experiences, adventures and creative discovery. From Banjul to Chennai and many stops in between, Sue has coupled her travel with her passion for local crafts and goods. She finally landed in Austin, Texas, and first began sharing her creations with family and friends, then shoppers at large. Her design company, Susan Malcik ATX, speaks of being a solopreneur firmly rooted in Austin; however, her designs and materials speak of exotic places, exotic traditions and worldly travels.

Growing up in Houston, Susan never thought of herself as an entrepreneur. After completing her formal education, she began a job as a publishing assistant at The Houston Gardener, a resource for all things "green" in the Houston area. Then came love and marriage and a move to Austin.

When she arrived in Austin, she took the knowledge she had gained while working in the publishing business in Houston and established a monthly newspaper called The Austin Garden Press. Sue was a one-woman whirlwind of advertising sales, writing, photography,

SHE Susan

distribution and marketing. The periodical filled the need for pre-internet information for the large gardening community, and it was wildly successful, but when domestic necessity required her to be employed (she was purchasing a house), she left AGP on the shelf. Over the next three years, she worked for a printing company, soaking up all they had to offer in the realm of design. Her creative spirit and ability to think like a customer made her a natural.

A long-held dream of Susan and her husband's was to experience the world through travel and employment in the U.S. foreign service. Initially they made the decision to enter the rarified air of the foreign service through the Peace Corps. Susan and her husband served four years in The Gambia, West Africa, where they worked in the Agriculture and Rural Development division and where Susan subsequently became training director. And so began the passion for seeking out and collecting local crafts, beads and fabrics. Markets and local sellers came to know Susan well and treated her as a most valued customer wherever and whenever she shopped.

After the four-year stint with the Peace Corps, Susan's husband landed a position with the foreign service, and thus began her mosaic of interesting positions in numerous embassies as a "trailing spouse" who had skills that could be used in whatever posting they held. India, Cameroon, Barbados, Senegal, Côte d'Ivoire, Djibouti, the U.S. and Germany were a few of the countries where Susan packed, unpacked and repacked her collection of antique, vintage and contemporary beads and fabrics. She created with some of them as she went, and she stored the rest for future construction and design. Over the almost 19 years that Susan's husband served at the various posts around the world she shopped, haggled, purchased and stored rare finds, Susan also held positions in various embassies in administrative roles.

She officially joined the State Department as an office management specialist in Kabul, Afghanistan, where she served for 14 months before rejoining her husband in Sweden. Afghanistan proved to be a rich source of crafts for her, and her collection grew again. In Sweden, she became office manager to the deputy chief of mission until both she and her husband returned to the U.S. for assignments stateside. The tons (literally) of beads, collectibles and fabrics were stored away while Susan was assigned to postings in Paris (where her husband retired) and finally in Chennai, India—the final leg of long careers for the couple.

Not only did furniture and personal belongings await them when they arrived back in Austin, but also the accumulation of purchases found during shopping expeditions in exotic countries all over the globe. It was time to begin to utilize all of the treasures collected over 35 years of travels. Susan went through all of the necessary exercises to set up and organize her business under the name Susan Malcik ATX. She established online accounts to sell her creations through Zazzle, Spoonflower, Society6 and Redbubble. Her website illustrates her jewelry and fabric designs, which showcase the vintage and antique beads and ethnic patterns discovered in many countries. The inspiration for her creativity

is the exotic textiles collected over the decades traveling the world. She also has transformed the colorful international designs into wallpapers, small accent furnishings and clothing. Susan has secured a spot in the San Antonio boutique Mockingbird Handprints, where many of her original works are found.

In addition to textile and jewelry design, Susan found an unplanned niche in the first quarter of 2020. Upon hearing of the need for masks for healthcare workers, and at the urging of a friend, Susan began to

construct masks that met clinical standards, using original fabrics of her design. Hundreds of masks of different styles were created, ordered, shipped and donated and/or sold throughout 2020, even providing wedding masks covered in lace and small pearls. As the demand for masks began to decline, Susan returned to jewelry design and construction, which, along with her graphic art, occupies her workdays. Plans for the future include greatly expanding her jewelry line and reorganizing her inventory of beads and fabrics. Susan has plans for the exotic vintage and antique beads that become more precious as the years go by. Seeing these treasures out of storage and onto the ears and necks of buyers makes Susan happy. She also plans to expand her jacket line, providing shopping opportunities for those who discover them in the San Antonio shop. Watching the world collide with Texas is a joy to behold!

Jessica

GARDNER MCCOY

Head Above Water LLC

Jessica McCoy is an incredible example of a young woman who had an idea, motivation and the nerve to take the plunge. It was the perfect move in starting a concierge swim school.

Jess is the poster child for having a dream, the drive and the savvy to get her new business up and running (and successful) very quickly. And in her own words, "You've got to allow yourself to try … and to fail"— but fail she has not. With a dual degree in sociology and English from Southern Methodist University, owning her own business was not in her sightline upon graduation in 2016. She had been a member of the SMU swim team but, as with most athletes at the end of the college career, the sport is set aside for "grown-up" activities. Like so many entrepreneurs, everything she did post-graduation added to her knowledge and experience in ways she could not have imagined.

Upon graduation, Jessica was immediately hired as a junior staff member, working with children at University United Methodist Church. She worked with staff and congregants, honing her myriad of presentation and one-on-one skills. As an obvious extrovert, Jess has the innate talent of establishing and maintaining relationships, which are important in any people-to-people business.

SHE
Jessica

After marrying her longtime boyfriend, she moved to a new environment in Midland, Texas, where he lived and worked. A new town, new friends and new work environment were no problem for Jess. She quickly found employment working as the development director for a nonprofit. When funding for this position ended, she quickly segued into sales positions within the oil and gas industry, which was the primary employer in the area. Given the volatility of the industry, Jess held several successful roles in sales before landing in a role juggling over 500 contract labor positions for a recruiting company. Once again, the industry slowed, and there was a layoff.

Often a layoff signals an ending and a disappointment; however, in reality, many people say a layoff was the best thing that ever happened to them because it became the motivator to rethink career, goals and purpose. Jess did just this. She had been casually offering swim lessons on a very part-time basis for over a year, and she took the opportunity of the layoff to rethink her personal and professional goals. She adored children, she had developed a wide network of friends with small children, she was a talented swimmer and she had honed her skills working with the public during her residency in pastoral care at UUMC.

She did her homework, researching business ownership and all of the elements she would need. She sought counsel from a lawyer, an accountant and others in business. She made a list of questions and checked off all of the necessary tasks and opened Head Above Water LLC in the spring of 2020. She had decided that she wanted to be selective in the

number of clients, the schedule she wanted to maintain, the ages of her students and the season she would operate. She also determined that she wanted to provide the highest level of service and support, so she created a concierge style of school. Her business model allows parents to have access to her beyond the weekly skills lessons she provides to the children. Additional support includes consultations on water safety at home, at public pools, recreational water sports and any situation where water safety is a concern.

Her school is beginning its second year in operation and has a 99% return rate for repeat students. Her primary concern is not about the operation or success of the business but about the safety of kids around water, whether they are with her in class or enjoying recreation with their family. Because of this, she provides all safety training to the parents and to the children.

Twenty-four/seven availability for parents' questions and concerns involving water sports can be challenging. As a wife and mom of two,

Jessica lives a very full life. She relies heavily on technology for marketing through social media and her website to allow for ease of scheduling class sessions. She insists on time for herself early in the day, as her alone time to drink a cup of tea and mindfully set her intentions for the day. She reserves time for herself to renew and regenerate, which keeps her relaxed and focused on the needs of her and her family.

Jessica believes in following your passion, believing in yourself and building a support team that will provide you with answers to questions.

SHE

Jessica

And most importantly, allowing yourself to try. She believes you can never really know until you take a risk. She believes women do exceptionally well in leadership roles because they think about the big picture and are acutely empathetic—both attributes have helped her build a strong and thriving business within its first year. Questions come up when starting any new business. Newbie business owners can create so many questions that movement toward an actual beginning is stalled or even shut down. Jessica knew this. She gathered information, did research and then began. As she wisely says, "It is important to allow yourself to try and to fail. But the important thing is to try."

Carmaleta
MCKINNIS-WILLIAMS

*Proverbs 31 Consulting
Enterprise LLC*

Carmaleta lives her personal mission, whether in the corporate world, in personal relationships or focused on her 2-year-old business as a racial equity ambassador and workshop facilitator. She considers herself a work in progress, and that work has led her to launch a consulting business which is a reflection of her mission—so much so that she named the firm Proverbs 31 Consulting.

Contemporary interpretation of the Bible's Proverbs chapter 31 describes a woman who is a leader and honors God. She is able to take stock of any situation, make meaningful decisions and manage activities to a positive outcome and then she moves forward to do it again and again. Carmaleta fully embodies and encourages some of the many characteristics of Proverbs 31 women in her consulting relationships. She is faithful, strong, well-rounded and charitable. She is honorable, wise and kind. Carmaleta is all of these qualities, and she encourages them in her work. Through Proverbs 31 Consulting, she uses her real-life experience to help organizations expand multicultural awareness. With a focus on community engagement, relationship-building and leadership development, she helps organizations build healthy, equitable enterprises to include all staff/members.

Carmaleta grew up in Detroit, Michigan, in a loving, supportive family and, like many individuals in the area, began a career in the automotive industry. Along the way, she earned a bachelor's degree in communications and a Master of Business Administration. No matter her professional title, her roles with General Motors for 28 years included customer care and relationship-building. While at GM, Carmaleta was founder and leader of the South-Central Region Women's Network. This group was organized to assist women with professional development resources and create leadership opportunities. With her background in marketing, customer care and leadership development, Carmaleta was able to support and mentor others as they advanced professionally.

Mentors and role models are critical to a career. Finding a female role model has been difficult in many professions, especially those historically dominated by men. In past years, young girls have been presented with many images that are defined strictly as feminine. Girls were encouraged to become teachers, nurses and other supporting roles, with very few suggestions of options such as director, manager, leader, CEO or president. Over the years, companies have come to realize that the talent and abilities provided by women have been overlooked. Fortunately, times they are a-changin'. Female role models are critical for women who choose to enter the workforce. If they can't look up and see women who have been successful, they are less likely to be successful themselves. The presence of women in leadership positions and the opportunity to network with them and learn from them are vital to helping motivate women to advance. A study from New York University indicates that

89% of women tend to set more ambitious goals when they have been mentored or inspired by others rather than going it alone.

In 2018, Carmaleta felt it was time to take a chance and leave the corporate world to focus on doing what she does best on her own and in her own way. Proverbs 31 Consulting was born. All of the passion she carried into her various positions at GM and in her outside activities would now be focused on helping others directly in their own small businesses. One conversation at a time, Carmaleta began to help others bring their dreams to life and their products and services to market. Her years working within a world-class business gave her plenty of background for leading startups toward success. Life was good and business was good.

And then 2020 arrived. Carmaleta has provided extensive involvement, support and mentorship of women and women of color outside of her consulting business. She is a member of Leadership Austin, Impact Austin, the City of Austin's Equity Action Team, the advisory board for Solar Austin, the Travis County Sheriff's Department Community Outreach Program: Building Bridges Community Dialogue, and the National Black MBA Association: Mentor-Coach, and Leaders of Tomorrow. And in her free time, she became an ordained minister.

SHE *Carmaleta*

As the artist Frida Kahlo said, "At the end of the day, we can endure much more than we think we can." It is disappointing to be on a success trajectory and have a speed bump occur; however, women are known for their resilience, and Carmaleta is no exception. When the unexpected arrives, individuals with infinite thinking look at the situation as an opportunity. Because Carmaleta has a sense of purpose, which is to inspire others to become all that they can become, she knows that her superpowers lie in more than just helping small businesses grow and thrive. She can be the voice that needs to be heard and share her wisdom (another Proverbs 31 attribute) to help others understand the importance and value of inclusion. As the 2020 pandemic grew, the Black Lives Matter movement began to unfold, and Carmaleta found herself in a different role in Proverbs 31 Consulting. Rather than assisting others in growing their bottom line, she began to provide mentorship in diversity, equity and inclusion. She was asked to assist Austin Health Commons (AHC), whose mission is to help the city of Austin become a healthy and healed community. AHC is a nonprofit organization that cultivates root cause community healing (in part) through a process called Truth, Racial Healing and Transformation. Carmaleta has also been called to provide training, workshops and lectures to assist a variety of groups in racial healing. She is currently serving as an equity mentor and providing diversity training for multiple organizations. In this way, her pivot is meaningful.

Declared "awesome" by the most amazing husband on the planet, Carmaleta McKinnis-Williams shares the message of the value of communication. Not just within our everyday circles but by being courageous and reaching outside of our personal bubbles. She leaves everyone with the message, "Talk to someone you wouldn't normally speak with. Know someone different. Learn from others."

Aditi
MERCHANT

Big & Mini

Business ideas can take years to percolate in the minds of fledgling entrepreneurs, or they can appear to take form overnight. Big & Mini, created by Aditi Merchant and two friends, falls into the latter category. With a passion for turning lemons into lemonade, coupled with the smarts of engineering students, they launched their business almost overnight.

In 2020, the University of Texas and thousands of other schools were closed for in-person classes due to COVID-19. With this came enforced isolation, which hit the college community hard. We think of 20-somethings as the most "connected" generation in existence; however, numerous studies show that millennials are the loneliest generation. Polls have found that almost 50% of Gen Zers (18-22) said they always or often feel lonely, compared to 30% of millennials (22-38), while baby boomers are the least lonely. Loneliness has been identified as a new epidemic in modern U.S. society. Add the effects of a pandemic and self-imposed isolation to these findings during normal times, and Aditi and her fellow engineering students felt there was an urgent need for connection. Social distancing and the closure of businesses and gathering places were compounding the intense feelings of isolation for all age groups.

As a high school student, Aditi was a regular visitor to senior assisted living centers, where she entertained by playing her flute and simply being a listening ear for the residents. She also served as a youth coach, mentoring on subjects from robotics to financial literacy. Knowing the value of connection between all ages, she found herself looking for a solution during a time when most everyone, young and old, was alone and lonely.

As a University of Texas sophomore majoring in biomedical engineering, Aditi was well-equipped to implement her idea with her colleagues. An honors student in her first year at UT, Aditi designed a symptom-tracking app for children with chronic diseases, and a medical device sterilization tool for low-resource countries. She is no stranger to innovation. Her newest creation, Big & Mini, is an online platform that connects college students and seniors through virtual communication. By matching vetted students and seniors with similar interests, connections are made and relationships are formed. In less than one year, Big & Mini grew to over 1,500 users in 50 states. The "Bigs" and the "Minis" all report successful relationships growing through their virtual interactions. A boost in visibility came in the form of media stories in the Houston Chronicle, Parade Magazine and exposure on the "Today" show.

As a child, Aditi was fascinated with disparate relationships in every part of her life, whether academic or just for fun. She was in the habit of constructing things—from a duct-tape dress to a camera made from popsicle sticks. She loved European history and robotics, coding camps

SHE Aditi

and ecology. She found her special talent to be gathering seemingly unrelated ideas and stirring them all together to make sense in a practical way. Helping her fellow humans is her passion, fueled by her ingenuity and creativity. Aditi is a highly motivated college sophomore who has brainstormed and launched a successful business in a matter of months. How is this different than so many other new female entrepreneurs?

According to one study, millennials and Gen Zers are more likely to start a business than those in older generations. Baby boomers, for example, tend to launch their first business at an average age of 35. Younger generations start their first business around age 27, implying they're more eager to start businesses and possibly are more willing to take risks in doing so. And the age is dropping.

Surveys suggest that millennials and Gen Zers value entrepreneurship and startups more than generations past valued them, with the majority of millennials admiring entrepreneurs and loving the idea of being self-employed. Over 62% of millennials have considered starting their own business, with 72% feeling that startups and entrepreneurs are a necessary economic force for creating jobs and driving innovation. Nearly one in three millennials (30%) said they have some type of small business or side hustle, with 19% saying it's their main source of income. A majority (54%) of those in Gen Z indicate they aspire to owning their own business. This age group is positioned to be the most entrepreneurial generation yet. A Gallup poll indicates that 77% of Gen Z students want to be their own boss; 45% intend to run their own business and 42% aim to invent something that will transform the world. While millennials set the trend of job-hopping and side hustles, Gen Zers are focused on working for themselves and only for themselves. Women have a significant role in this trend.

Growth opportunities for women are increasing in all professions as well as in business startups. In the past, women who sought to break out of the mold of traditional female roles in business had to "go it alone" without financing or mentors. That is not the case in today's climate. New programs such as The LaunchPad helped Aditi and her partners.

The LaunchPad is a program in the School of Undergraduate Studies at the University of Texas that helps students in all disciplines explore entrepreneurship at their own pace in cross-disciplinary environments. The owners of Big & Mini received a fellowship as well as guidance and mentorship as they began their business. Subsequently, they became plugged into the Kendra Scott Women's Entrepreneurial Leadership Institute, where they found additional support. Aditi was a Female Featured Founder in 2020, joining the likes of numerous enthusiastic women entrepreneurs who are headed for success.

Aditi is only beginning. Within the next five years, she knows that Big & Mini will have revolutionized how elders and college students connect. And along the way, she will enjoy the support of powerful female role models who have preceded her while growing into one herself.

Wanda
MONTEMAYOR

Community Arts LLC

Powerful components of many women-owned businesses are, of course, leadership and relationship-building. In some businesses, this may look like relationships with clients, employees or, on a larger scale, a community (local or global). Project management is closely tied to communication, team-building and effective leadership. Many studies find that women possess innate qualities that provide effective leadership of companies and large-scale projects. Wanda Montemayor is a superior example of the integration of her passion, her business and these innate qualities of relationship development. She has included her Austin community as an integral part of her professional life. It is almost impossible to determine where her chosen career as a licensed therapist intersects with an embrace of and involvement with the Austin community.

As Wanda says, "Community art therapy is about creating a relationship with the community and being able to see it—that public art piece. It gives you a voice that you can see. When you see your message, it has a deeper meaning." Although her primary practice is to serve as a licensed therapist, Wanda has involved hundreds of individuals in her projects over the past decade.

Her first employment was as an art teacher at Sarah Lively Middle School. Being the multitasking genius she is, Wanda also began her march toward receiving a graduate degree in counseling at Texas State during her teaching career. Upon completion, she began her role as counselor at Fulmore before transferring to O'Henry Middle School, where she remained until 2021.

During her time at Lively Middle School, she instructed at-risk students and established an after-school art enrichment program. As a teen mom, Wanda had chosen a career as an art teacher, which connected her passion for art and provided the flexibility to be a fully engaged parent.

During her 10 years at Lively Middle School, she either established or directed programs, such as campus career day, a teacher mentor program and a liaison with Big Brothers. As a counselor, she conducted the first of many massive projects involving more than individual students.

Realizing that students were somewhat limited to using only paint as individual artistic expression, she introduced the creation of mosaic tiles, which were then incorporated into community murals. In this way, not only were art students involved, but also she could gather together the entire school community to create beautiful works of art. Wanda's feeling was that by making mosaic tiles, the students would create art that would exist longer than a moment—it would endure. By creating art and beautifying their school, these involved students would make lasting impressions and build a sense of empowerment within themselves.

This was the beginning of Wanda's community art projects and also a turning point in her career. As Wanda moved from art teacher to counselor and art therapist, she, like so many, experienced the unfolding of her life's purpose. She began to realize that her passion included creating beautiful pieces of art and watching the healing and sense of personal pride that unfolds with a community project. This realization was pivotal in her decision to pursue a license in art therapy. While at Lively Middle School, Wanda organized and led groups through the completion of five painted murals, eight water fountain projects and five mosaic murals. The most prominent and well-known project was a mosaic on the most public face of the school on South Congress Avenue.

In 2009, Wanda moved to O'Henry Middle School, where she served in a part-time capacity as an art therapist. She led group and individual counseling and provided academic services. Each year she directed student-led mosaic projects on campus, which add to the aesthetics of the campus and also provide students an opportunity to participate in large-scale mosaic installations. The tiles for all of the projects were handmade, glazed and installed by the students. She also supervised graduate student interns who provided thousands of hours of direct services to the children in areas of loss and grief, domestic violence, sexual trauma, anger management, social skills, incarceration issues and self-esteem building. Wanda has lived out her life's purpose in creating art, building community and serving the needs of the next generation. Completed art projects now number 10 and appear in the administration office, corridors, student areas and on the wall of the campus entrance.

During her tenure at O'Henry Middle School, Wanda also opened a private counseling practice to serve clients outside of the public school community. She specializes in art therapy, play therapy, and Eye Movement Desensitization and Reprocessing, as well as traditional counseling modalities.

Outside of the school and private practice communities, Wanda has also directed or co-directed large community mosaic projects at parks and community centers. Although directing mosaic mural installations in 2013 (Windmill Run's *Phoenix Rising*), 2015 (Barton Hills Community Park *We Are Barton Hills*) and 2017 (YMCA Town Lake *Nuestro Arte*) have fulfilled dreams of making community art, perhaps the largest and most prominent installation is the 2011 Deep Eddy Pool mural, which Wanda co-directed. This community project includes 1,200 square feet of handmade clay tiles (six tons of clay), each etched with a piece of the

overall mural as well as personal messages and mirrored colored glass. Community volunteers, organized and co-led by Wanda, created these tiles in over 20 workshops. Thousands of volunteers contributed to the project over four years of planning and installation It tells the story of the historic Deep Eddy Pool. A PBS documentary "Mosaic-The Deep Eddy Mural" was created in 2012 to tell the full story of the art, the passion, the people and the commitment to creating this piece of community art.

Through listening to her art, pursuing her passion and utilizing her skills of people engagement, Wanda Montemayor and her gifts are serving again, again and yet again.

Chi

NDIKA

Luv Fats

Chi Ndika eats ice cream every day and is passionate about every bite. Although Chi is not vegan, she produces varieties of a vegan dessert she has branded Luv Fats, the most scrumptious frozen treat ever tasted. And it is made with "luv" from start to finish.

When asked, some company leaders either cannot articulate their purpose or believe their raison d'etre is to make a lot of money and/or be their own boss. From the outset, Chi was very clear that the fuel that started the Luv Fats engine was love. In 2017, Chi wanted to create a special birthday treat for her mom, who had discovered she had a dairy allergy. What better celebratory offering than ice cream that contains no dairy? As someone who loves baking and cooking, Chi dove into creative mode and began a trial-and-error process of creating something tasty. Very important to the process was the feel on her tongue. It needed to have the taste, and Chi knew the texture was a critical factor. She wanted to use an ingredient other than bananas to provide the creaminess. The birthday arrived, and mom was thrilled. Chi knew she was onto something, and she continued to experiment with her recipe. In 2018, when friends started to ask her to recreate her dessert for their events, Luv Fats was born.

SHE *Chi*

Passion is what drives a business to succeed. Many aspiring entrepreneurs do not have a passion for their businesses, and without substantial financial backing, they are not always willing to do the necessary difficult work. Some newly minted business owners do not even have the passion for making money. They just like the idea of success. Chi Ndika does not fall into either of these categories. She knows that creating new recipes, producing Luv Fats and marketing and selling are all hard work, but she is up for it. She says she cannot imagine doing anything else.

Chi is committed to creating her confection with the best ingredients possible. She sources all of them locally, conceiving new and unique pairings from what is available during each season. Although cookies and crème is a perennial favorite, she adds a hint of lavender when in season to produce a heavenly taste. Her creativity is endless, and shoppers never know what new flavors will appear at the Mueller Farmers' Market or the variety of restaurants and shops where she personally stocks the coolers with Luv. Chai and chocolate, yellow watermelon sorbet, Kenyan coffee, butter pecan, hibiscus orange and pandan fluff are only a few of the flavors. Chi's creativity is obvious, but she is also inspired by what she discovers amongst the booths at the farmers market.

SHE

Chi

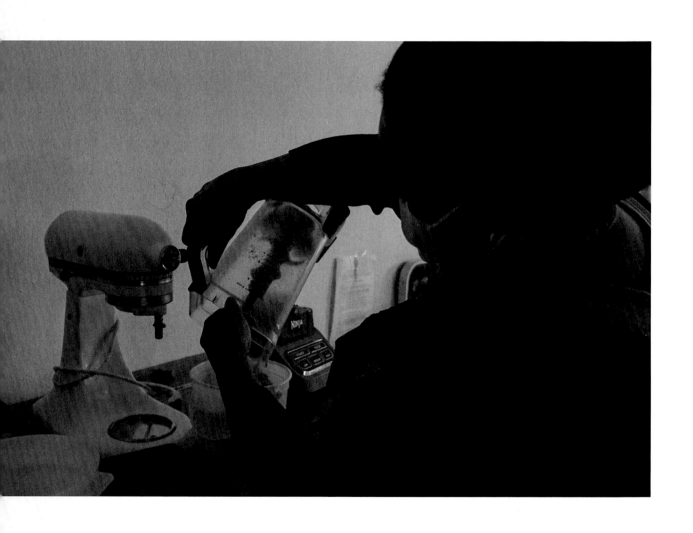

Advisors in the food industry indicate that, while the ice cream industry is a fun business to be in, it often takes incredible capital to get into. Sometimes it's best not to pay attention to advisors and just do what you love while being cautious. Chi did not take out a loan or seek investors when she was starting her business. She did not even apply for a credit card. She sought out cost-effective ways to begin bootstrapping through the process. By seeking out low-cost ways to source materials, commercial facilities to produce and then a farmers market to sell, she was able to easily launch, building as she went. The market gave her access to the demographic of ice cream lovers she felt would taste and repeat buy her product, and she was right. Once customers tasted Luv and came back week after week, she knew she had made the right decision to leave her job as an office manager at a nonprofit and follow her heart. Food industry consultants also advise newbie frozen treat business owners to acquire lots of equipment before starting to produce. Again, this advice isn't always right for every situation. Chi started small, making small batches and packaging in pints without the need for vast amounts of equipment. She continues to produce weekly in small batches, with capacity expanding as she acquires more production space and more equipment, but always staying conservative.

Although COVID-19 slowed many businesses, the demand for ice cream was constant, and the request for healthy options has been growing. Luv Fats is celebrated by vegans and non-vegans alike. In the past, Chi and her helpers (often her mom) offered small samples at farmers markets, but due to temporary COVID-19 restrictions, these were no longer allowed.

Chi started her business with an idea based on the love of family, and she continues to find love as a source for infusing good vibes into every batch of Luv Fats. She knows she needs to be in the right mindset to create and to churn, so she approaches each production run with a good attitude of love and gratitude. Her batches are small, and quality control is key. Cold packing (outsourcing of production in large batches) is currently not an option, as she is mindful of keeping the quality high and the taste/texture perfect. A brick-and-mortar shop is a possibility, as she loves the atmosphere of small ice cream shops, especially with her family at her side, supporting her and occasionally working alongside her. Luv Fats started as a family vision and will continue as one.

With the demanding business of ice cream production and all that it takes to bring the delicious goodness to market, Chi works to take care of herself through yoga, walking, stretching and getting plenty of rest. Her days start early and can be long, depending on the production schedule for the week. She is a strong believer in the Austin economy and works to support other local businesses like hers. Being a presence in the local community, she is able to discover other women of color who she can help support.

For now, fear of the future does not exist in Chi's vocabulary. She is enthusiastic, creative, kind and driven. Because Luv is her vision.

Chi

Lorie
NEWMAN

Hair by Lorie Newman

Lorie is a stylist who has created gorgeousness in hair and makeup for fashion events, private clients, weddings and other special occasions. Many of her clients have been a part of her life for many years. And giving back … that importance of generosity … has always been a part of her life and her profession. It is as natural as the creativity which guides her hands to provide just the right advice, just the right style or just the right look tailored to the individual—whether men or women. Although there are many outstanding attributes of business owners, we typically think of adjectives such as *creative, enterprising* and *clever* to describe them. These are all very true of Lorie Newman; however, she's also considered to be generous in her personal life as well as her business life. This is key to her personal mission and satisfaction.

As entrepreneur and marketing strategist Leo Bogee advises, "We hear a lot about the qualities needed for great business leadership—confidence, passion, integrity—but there's one critical quality that doesn't get nearly enough attention, in my opinion: *Generosity.* It's kind of counterintuitive, if you think about it. Isn't the instinct to give things away at odds with the goal of business: to get more and more? Not at all. That's the paradox that great business leaders naturally understand."

SHE *Lorie*

As with so many business founders and owners, Lorie did not start her career in her ideal profession. The nine-to-five world of banking did not suit her personality nor her ability to create and define her role as a significant player in the lives of others. As a wife and mom of three, she knew there was something more in tune with her natural abilities and passion. As a child, Lorie was close to her grandmother, who would allow Lorie to accompany her into the weekly feminine world of the beauty shop. This was a place of community, talk and laughter. The experience served as an environment for the uplifting of spirits when hair was washed (sometimes permed or colored), set in excruciatingly prickly hair rollers and placed under the dryer away from the world of responsibility and needy families. It was a purely feminine institution. Lorie was fascinated and knew she liked that environment. She was instructed by her grandma to "never leave the house undone," and this directive stuck. Even now, Lorie is never "undone."

After leaving the banking world, Lorie quickly powered through cosmetology school in 11 months. She was on a mission to get to her perfect destination. As a freshly minted graduate, she did her homework and found the top three prestigious salons in Austin where she felt she would be "at home" as a creative who cared about her profession and her clients. She interviewed and was immediately offered positions at all three. She knew that all three were looking for talent and skills, as well as the drive to succeed.

SHE *Lorie*

Lorie remained for 11 years at her salon of choice, building a reputation and a solid, loyal client base. Eventually, she knew it was time to start on her own. Rather than developing her own salon with all of the attention-grabbing situations that go along with it, Lorie decided to become an independent stylist. In this way, she could focus on using her skills to create and have the independence to choose her clients, services and schedule. She knew the initial year would be the most challenging while she built her business, but she was committed to marketing, networking and doing what she does best—finding ways to share with others in need. She was generous with her time and generous with her business cards.

Lorie has since spent the last decade in her own business, setting her own standards and rules. She has aligned with salon owners with whom she contracts for space as a home base for her business. While serving clients in Austin in the salon, she also takes commissions that allow her to travel.

Lorie is very thankful for her family and husband who have been supportive of her dream from the beginning. Having family support is crucial to the success of any new business. And in this success, Lorie has also found easy outlets for the generosity that fuels her, equal to her creativity. Friends and colleagues describe Lorie in two words … talented and giving. She has frequently provided haircuts to adults and children who cannot afford them and generously donates her time and talents to the Boys and Girls Club as well as an organization affiliated with Dell Children's Hospital, Beautifully Loved. This organization focuses its attention on teens (primarily) who are undergoing or have undergone cancer treatment. Although it provides support throughout the year, the annual fashion show, a fundraiser, also provides the teens with a boost in self-esteem by featuring them as models, complete with promotional photo shoots, hip and trendy teen styles, and hair and makeup sessions to get them ready for the show. They are the stars, and Lorie is a large part of the planning and execution of the event.

Because she sets her own goals, appointments and schedule, Lorie can choose to work just as hard as she wishes. She takes time off for self-care at the gym and for travel, but she is also ready to be available when a client (her clients become her family) is in need, whether in Austin or elsewhere. Helping clients who have lost hair through cancer treatment is not unusual for Lorie. She has become knowledgeable on the quality and styling of wigs and has worked with clients to make the best choices for them as they suffer the effects of chemotherapy.

Above all, Lorie's motivation is not only to be a creative stylist, but also to help others, whether they are clients or other stylists who might need support. It is important for her to be in a profession she loves and to be available to those in need. The Huffington Post reports that generosity is good for you. It leads to better health, less stress, stronger relationships and even a longer life. Adopting an attitude of generosity is not only good for health, but it is good for business … although some, like Lorie Newman, radiate it naturally.

Katarzyna
PRIEBE

Priebe Security Services, Inc.

"*It may seem incongruous* to link security services with relationships. At first blush, when we think of armed guards and nightly patrol officers, we do not imagine that the founder/owner of the company puts relationship-building at the top of her list of values. Katarzyna Priebe never hesitates when explaining that the core value of her business is to "build enduring relationships … one customer, one employee at a time." And for her, these words are not the typical hollow obligatory phrase posted on a website. She lives it and breathes it and has done so since the first day of operation in 2005. And this is no secret. This is clearly how Katarzyna approaches every single interaction. A client reports that, as a new service provider, Katarzyna worked tirelessly to accommodate her special staffing requests. Handling special requests has always been common practice for the staff of Priebe Security, that considers "special" treatment standard operating procedure.

Katarzyna immigrated to the United States when she was 13 and quickly became immersed in American culture and the American dream. Her father was a role model who always sought to own and operate his own restaurant, although it never came to be. After graduating from the University of Texas at Austin with a degree in Russian and hoping to be an interpreter, she realized that relocation would be essential. At the time, she believed it best to stay in Texas, so she continued the sales

SHE *Katarzyna*

career which she had started while attending university. Being a conscientious and eager learner, she sought to absorb every bit of knowledge she could about the business. Not imagining herself as a business owner initially, Katarzyna worked in sales for security companies that provided services in Austin and internationally. She paid attention from day one, learning all she could about the operations and products of the company, so she could be the best provider of services for the customers—who ultimately became friends. If there was a question about any aspect of the company, she wanted to be able to provide her customers with answers. Her last place of employment before deciding it was time to make her move was a very large international company, which provided quality service, yet something was missing for Katarzyna. It seemed to be that focus on enduring relationships that meant so much to her.

In 2004, she closed the door on her life as an employee and began to wear the title of founder and owner of Priebe Security Services. First steps are not always easy, yet they are exciting. She believed she knew what quality services were lacking in her service area of Austin, Texas, and her company would focus on the wants and needs of the customer and the care of her staff.

Although women-owned businesses are on the rise, Katarzyna is one of approximately 2% of women who develop successful operations in trade and service industries. And the number of women who start full-service security companies focusing on direct guard and patrol services is even smaller. For Katarzyna, the exact services provided were less of a concern than ensuring customer and employee care.

The Global Entrepreneurship Monitor reports that opportunity, rather than necessity, fuels women in starting their own companies. Women under the age of 35 are reported as being open to changing jobs, changing careers and taking on challenges in the types of products and services in their new businesses. Statistics indicate that women in older age groups often stay where they are until a change of life situation necessitates a change in career, prompting them to open their thinking to new opportunities. Layoffs, company shutdowns or shifts in family situations often fuel the creative fire to begin something new. For Katarzyna, opportunity and desire to do things differently paved the way to Priebe Security.

Katarzyna has always felt that whatever happens within her company, paying attention to relationships is key. She knows her promise, her word and her reputation are on the line. As the head of marketing and sales, Katarzyna will never do or say anything just to close a deal. Integrity and impeccable ethics guide every interaction.

Although she started out as a "one-woman show" and has now grown to over 300 staff members, Katarzyna considers herself a small company. It is important for her to ensure that the company values are firmly entrenched in every interaction, every shift, every conversation. Having a larger professional staff now means that she does not respond to every call on her cell phone and that when a staff member is not available, she does not don her own uniform and go out on patrol. An adequately sized staff, extensive training and an excellent management team mean that she's no longer on "official" 24/7 call.

In addition to creating enduring relationships with customers, Katarzyna believes it is vital to provide the best work environment possible. She has been told by prospective staff that they know who (in the business) cares for their employees, and her company is one of the best. Katarzyna seeks to create an environment where each employee is respected and treated like the professionals that they are. According to Inc. Magazine, small women-owned businesses are 1.7 times more productive than their male counterparts. Women business owners prove to be much better at leading their teams—they take the time to see their employees as whole people, not just "worker bees." Although business owners may say they know their employees well, citing examples of knowing spouse names and/or employee hobbies, the owners may have no idea what a staff member's inner values/goals/hopes/dreams/professional plans might be. In a small business, getting to know (*well*) the lifeblood of the company—the employees—is crucial. Not only does Katarzyna place profound importance on her office staff and guards, she worries about them and their safety as they go about their jobs. The bigger the service area and customer base, the bigger the worry. Her concern extends to their physical safety, making sure that the right people are in the right roles and that all of the right processes are in place. She gives her all to provide security for her customers, her employees and their families, and to make sure they know that these enduring relationships are the driving force before every moment of every interaction.

Veronica
SCHNITZIUS

American Leather Operations LLC

Veronica Schnitzius is the president of a large furniture manufacturing company headquartered in Dallas, Texas. American Leather Operations LLC employs over 400 people. Although her story is not one of ownership, she is a model of the commitment to education for herself and for others she influences—and of putting in the hard work leading to her goals and success. She lives and models a leadership role which highlights how to achieve success in whatever manner one might choose.

Often, there has been an erroneous notion that a successful, authentic female leader is a rare find. In decades past, women seeking to get ahead were directed to adapt to traditional schools of thought and follow the lead of their male counterparts. Act tough, have no close relationships in the workplace, keep your eye on the prize (growth and significant bottom line) and above all, closet away all of those feminine traits that will only show one to be weak. Make decisions, both business and personal, looking at male examples as a guide. Ignore innate talents, which might be deemed "soft." Women leaders sometimes felt they needed to choose between family and success in the workplace. None of these choices were considerations when focusing on the success of a male leader. He puts in the time, does the work, succeeds and advances. Too often, a woman's success was examined through the lens of what she had to "give up" or hide in order to rise to the top. Also, in years past, while a woman was nudged to act more like her male counterparts, a woman might be described as "clawing her way to the top," or "acting like a man" in order to be successful. This was often seen in a negative light. Do this to get ahead, but be careful when you do because you will be called less-than-flattering names behind your back. Although small instances of this attitude still exist, fortunately, it is no longer the typical one. Veronica has progressed through her career as her authentic self to rise to the role of President. She believes that by leading from her strength of education, training and authentic qualities of respect and caring, her progress and success are worthy of being emulated by others, as well as by her daughter.

Veronica grew up and was educated in Medellin, Colombia, as the daughter of a mother who served as a role model of a strong work ethic. With much danger and local violence as a backdrop for her family, and a father who was not in the picture, her mom was her example of overcoming adversity and how paying attention can lead to achieving good outcomes. Veronica excelled in school in order to make her mom proud and to prove that she would not follow in the steps of a father who suffered from addiction (he subsequently achieved recovery, attended college and became a CPA).

At the same time as she was completing her undergraduate degree in industrial engineering, Veronica studied intensive English and then began an internship at a furniture manufacturing firm in Dallas. She returned to Colombia and worked at the accounting firm of Klynveld Peat Marwick

SHE Veronica

Goerdeler while awaiting a visa to return to the U.S. She met and married her first husband, a physician who moved to the U.S. The marriage ended shortly thereafter, and Veronica began work at American Leather. The founder of the company hired her and two other individuals to improve processes on the production floor. This was difficult at first, as she was a 23-year-old woman, and the majority of the staff on the floor were men and older. Being in the minority is often a difficult situation to overcome. This setting requires confidence and skill in navigating the daily world in manufacturing. Initially she managed four people, but as she was promoted to maintenance manager, she was tasked with 45 direct reports.

Her ability to achieve goals, make positive changes and be respected translated to promotion after promotion. When she became assistant production manager, her supervisor recommended she continue her education by earning a master's in business administration. After her direct boss and mentor retired, she was promoted to vice president of operations and began a one-year leadership program at the urging of the owner of the company. In 2009 while in the leadership program, she began to run and signed up for the Chicago Marathon. Advantages of all the running? Less stress, better health and she met her second husband, Scott. She ran and entered four more marathons over another three years before switching to triathlons. During her running and training, she became pregnant, and when her daughter was eight months old, Veronica began training for a Half Ironman.

In 2011, Veronica was promoted to chief operating officer and then in 2017, she became president, the position she currently holds. Of great importance to Veronica is the effect she can have on the company, the staff and her family. She is aware that her employees see the progress she has made in the U.S. from intern to president of a company and have used her as a role model for their own families. She is aware of employees and their families seeking post-high-school education to create better lives for themselves. She firmly believes in education and knows that her story stands as an example for others to know what is possible.

Living by example is a mark of a true leader. Veronica knows that the employees are the company's largest asset, and diversity is a part of the culture. Men and women from 35 different countries are employed, visible in the flags of all countries displayed in the company café. The company has grown in size and scope and successfully navigated the challenges of the 2020 pandemic. Her leadership style emphasizes family and wellness. An area of the manufacturing plant is set aside for monthly employee events, a wellness center and other supportive services. She also sponsors children from her home country of Colombia to attend college. Education is critical.

Engaging with employees on the production floor is not unusual for this busy president. She knows that her staff look to her to set an example for "work family" interaction and support. She welcomes new ideas and innovations and listens to suggestions they have for improvements in products and the work environment. She believes that asking for feedback is important, but a willingness to hear criticism is also crucial. When asked how she leads, Veronica quickly answers, "By example."

When asked if there is anyone or any group she wishes to influence the most by example, Veronica quickly states that it's her daughter. Being a role model to employees is important, but it is also important to influence the next generation. Women can achieve executive positions through education, hard work and being their authentic selves. Women do not have to attempt to emulate male leaders, or any other leaders, for that matter. By using their innate skills and qualities, women can achieve personal and professional success. Lead by example authentically.

Joy
SELAK

JoyWrites

Joy Selak listens to the voice within. Some consider that voice intuition, divine guidance or our higher self; however, no matter what the source, being guided by inner wisdom is just as important as advisors and career counselors when it comes to navigating the professional path. We are called to set a clear course toward a profession after high school, but at that stage of life, are we always clear on our passion? What is our purpose? What can or should we do to serve mankind and ourselves? We often *think* we know.

As a young woman, Joy was clear. She completed a bachelor's degree, two master's degrees and a doctorate at Arizona State University. She followed her talents and interests in the field of education, specifically English, before diving into curriculum development … all a natural progression. After completing her graduate studies, Joy was selected to develop curricula in three school districts working for three different superintendents. The curriculum development covered kindergarten through 12th grade and was titled Blueprint for Communications. The Blueprint served as a roadmap for communication, with five areas of understanding in developmental learning. This large task took one year to develop, and it gave the school districts clear direction and also served to shape Joy in her thinking and how she views people.

As Joy completed the contract assignment for the school districts, she began to examine her next steps. She thoughtfully considered several career paths, setting specific goals and examining desires. She also looked to friends close to her and noticed that the most satisfied individuals were in the investment field working as stockbrokers. The facts that, at the time, this was a male-dominated field, had no ceiling on earnings and required no more degrees, all appealed to Joy. She interviewed with several firms, was offered positions with all of them and accepted the one with the best training and support. Over time as Joy became more successful, she moved from Arizona to California with her firm, met her husband who was also in investments and moved to his firm. Joy and her husband relocated their brokerage branch office to San Juan Island, Washington.

Through the years of rigorous education, decisions about the profession, relocations and all of the shifts, Joy was creative. Whether molding educational curricula to fit the needs of diverse school districts or assisting individuals in creating their investment strategies, Joy created. She states, "Writing is a magical wonder of letters, gathering them together to shape words and shaping words into stories, always looking for the positive." According to author Peter Drucker and other management scholars, innovation and creativity are inherent conditions for entrepreneurship. Creativity is "technically" inherited by everyone. It's more of a common human trait than a gift. In fact, a widely cited study by George Land, who founded a research and consulting institute to study the enhancement of creative performance, found that children are born creative but lose their creativity as they transition through life

and into adulthood. Scores of scientific papers indicate that if we can continue to exercise these creative muscles from childhood into our later years, we can continue to explore and enjoy the gift we were born with.

Joy is an example of this. As a financial advisor, she worked with clients to dream—often larger than they might have on their own. In this way, she assisted them in writing the script for happy endings to their personal and professional lives through their wise investments. Creativity comes in all shapes and forms.

SHE

Joy

While living with her husband on San Juan Island, Washington, Joy began to navigate the course of a long-term illness, which required many trips to the mainland to seek medical assistance. This illness and the story of healing ultimately found its way into her book titled "You Don't Look Sick," which offers support to others who find themselves in a similar life situation. She also authored an original play that was one of six winners at the San Juan Islands Playwrights Festival, winning the Audience Choice Award. This play was subsequently expanded to become an award-winning novel, "CeeGee's Gift."

Joy and her husband made the decision to relocate to Austin to be closer to quality medical professionals to help navigate health issues. Creativity continues to be central to Joy's life. As Joy states, "I've learned that having a chronic illness ... does not mean that I am useless and no longer have any gifts to share, but it may mean that I must develop some new ones." Since moving to Austin, Joy has written the second edition of her book on chronic illness (along with her physician); served as trustee and president of the board of directors of Zachary Scott Theater; served as development director for MINDPOP; served as trustee on global, national and local nonprofit boards; was founder of A Legacy of Giving and established JoyWrites, a website where she continues to gather letters to make words and shaping words into stories.

After receiving certification as a professional philanthropic advisor, Joy has aligned with nonprofits and individuals to create their personal giving plans. With experience gained and innate creativity and compassion, Joy collaborates with others to establish a story of philanthropy. She encourages communication about how they choose to share their resources. As Joy says, "Compelling stories are at the heart of philanthropy." Joy's creativity lives through her now and into the future through her communication, compassion and collaboration—qualities available to anyone.

Cassie

SHANKMAN

Sounds by Cassandra

Cassie Shankman is a woman with focus. From a young age, she has been in love with everything musical. Whether being called composer, orchestrator, teacher, pianist or music therapist, she is focused on all things music. She grew up in a family surrounded by arts and creativity. Her father believed in her and her musical abilities, encouraging her in school activities and extracurricular music groups. Cassie was inspired by her family and her teachers, who encouraged her to pursue music. Although her talents also lie in science and science competitions, Cassie pursued her music with a vengeance. All of her close friends were involved in music, especially the jazz band—a special love.

Upon graduation, Cassie attended the University of Texas at Austin, majoring in music composition. On her first day, she noticed that the program was populated by all men, with the exception of one female graduate student who became an inspiration for Cassie. Reassured by the grad student that she was not going it alone, she gained confidence and graduated ready to pursue her dreams. As a responsible young adult, Cassie believed she needed to retire educational debt before focusing on her music career entirely, so her first job was as a marketing coordinator while playing in a jazz trio as her side hustle. Utilizing her skills in social media marketing, Cassie worked for several businesses while playing and producing.

SHE *Cassie*

An opportunity to work as lead composer on movement tracks aligned her with the Center for Music Therapy. This organization and its staff composed and recorded music using brain-based music technology to assist people with damaged mobility. As this role ended, Cassie took the time to establish her own business, Sounds by Cassandra. She worked to incorporate music into every facet of her new endeavor. Whether she was composing or playing, every direction included music. She enjoyed the independence afforded by being her own boss, setting her own schedule and making things happen through her own efforts. The first step was to seek the advice of friends who could guide her as she became a full-time musician and business owner. As with all advice, some is helpful and some is not useful and can even send a newly minted business owner down a distracted path.

Her first year as a solo act (business owner, musician) was a solid success. Along with piano lessons and composing, Cassie began a full-time business as a DJ for parties, celebrations and some not-so-usual business events. She has discovered that there are a large number of opportunities and potential for what a DJ can do. She enjoys the people, the music and the opportunities to celebrate … but understands that DJing isn't all fun and games (and music). There is equipment to haul, long hours on her feet and a lot of social energy that goes into being the "life of the party." Appropriate amounts of downtime are crucial. From year one to year two, she almost doubled the number of gigs she booked. Marketing through word of mouth and social media helped grow her business.

SHE *Cassie*

As a woman in a male-dominated field, she was met with interesting comments. At a new event, she was often asked if she was the girlfriend of the DJ or if she was there to assist. She was sometimes told that she didn't look like a DJ and wondered what they thought she should look like! She also learned that, as a woman, she was sometimes expected to charge less than her male counterparts. As she's learned what comments to expect, she has learned not to be surprised. And to expect equal pay. She does not think of herself as a female DJ, but merely a great DJ. One benefit of being a great DJ, who happens to be female, is that she is often hired to entertain at female-empowerment events. And as a musician/composer, she is "in tune" with what is enjoyed and appropriate for each occasion. She doesn't let the difficulties of being a woman in a male-dominated profession hold her back from doing what she loves.

Male-dominated businesses are those that comprise 25% or fewer female full-time employees. In the U.S., only 7.2% of all women work full time in male-dominated businesses, and fewer are owners. Some women do not stay in these industries because, without mentors or role models, they often find it difficult to survive. There are higher stress levels for women (attitudes and comments, harassment and feelings of going it alone), and some women find it difficult to persist. Rather than leaving the industry, acting like "one of the guys" or being intimidated, women who succeed do as Cassie has done and find the silver lining. Being unique and looking for opportunities to capitalize on that uniqueness are what Cassie has done by marketing to women-specific events as well as her typical gigs.

Cassie admits she has learned a lot about herself as a business owner. She is kinder to herself and more understanding of what she needs and how to set boundaries. Entering into a challenging third year of business (2020) after having two incredibly successful years has taught her to make use of any downtime she has. Perfect her marketing and increase time spent in other areas such as teaching (even if it is online). She is careful to take care of herself and her needs. She believes that, although building a business requires a lot of focus and energy, it is not necessary

to overdo it to the point of exhaustion. There are various reasons why someone chooses to work for themselves, and the primary goal usually is to achieve happiness and satisfaction with the chosen profession. And Cassie knows that each person must define for her or himself just what that satisfaction, success and happiness might be. Listening to oneself is much more important than taking a cue from others.

Although she did not have a real vacation or significant time off from 2015 to 2020, she has learned that taking a mandatory pause in the hectic building of a business can be a blessing. By continuing to network and market, Cassie finds she is still very much in demand and booking for the future.

Marcia

SILVERBERG

HR Directions

Marcia Silverberg has been affectionately called a "badass" by a client of her company, and it is a moniker both affectionate and well-earned. When the client was asked to provide a review of her work, he summed it up in that one term. This self-possessed, well-put-together trainer of leaders, coach of executives and all-around go-to professional has worked with groups large and small to develop strategies to achieve difficult business goals.

Sometimes life situations are unexpectedly thrust upon an individual, and sometimes, as in Marcia's case, years of education, training and wisdom have positioned her for a successful transition from employee-leader to sole proprietor. Natural and smooth transitions to sole ownership may be the thing dreams are made of. Those first few months of going it alone can be frightening, but for Marcia, the transition was without hiccups.

 Recent research shows that between 2007 and 2016, the number of women-owned firms in the U.S. increased by 45%, compared to just a 9% increase among all businesses—five times the national average. Women leave the workforce for various reasons. These include having more control over their lives and schedules, having more flexibility in personal schedules and the ability to pay themselves more (ultimately!).

Marcia Silverberg made such a transition in 2013 from the corporate world to being her own boss, using the skills of past work environments to fine-tune her role as mentor/trainer/coach. After a dozen years serving as vice president and chief human resources officer for Ascension Health (the largest nonprofit healthcare system in the country with over 150,000 employees), Marcia left to focus her energies full time on the company she founded in 1998, HR Directions.

Marcia's love of organizational leadership led her to seek a Master of Social Work degree in organizational planning and leadership from Syracuse University, following her bachelor's in sociology and social work from the University at Albany, SUNY. She was drawn to this field of study early in life because the structure of an organization—the quality of its leaders and the commitment to mission, value and policies—directly affect the quality of its employees. The department that used to be called "personnel" then "human resources" has come to receive a bad rap because organizations often offload care of the employees to a group of individuals tasked with enforcing rules. Marcia has always affirmed that the groups she led were there to help the organization, not to be the department where employees are told, "NO!"

She believes that the environment is ripe for change in human resources (now often called People Management, Human Capital Management or People Operations), and she sees this happening in many organizations. What has been rule enforcement is now people enhancement. Marcia and her firm, HR Directions, provides support for organizations and their strategic development relating to both traditional and new approaches to care for staff. She has found that it's key to assist in all of the functions of what is often called people departments. HR is not an isolated department. It should be involved with the financial department and chief financial officer, as well as with the chief executive officer and throughout the organization.

Marcia's involvement in high school organizations and leadership in community groups on a grand scale was natural. Along with her professional activities, she has been heavily involved in community service on boards and executive committees and has served as chair of several groups. Her influence is extensive and includes Communities in Schools, Greater Austin Chamber of Commerce, Leadership Austin, LifeWorks, Seton Cove and United Way.

Most recently, she has expanded the executive coaching segment of her company. She works with various leadership groups to groom identified individuals who excel in their positions, with the goal of advancing in their organizations. She also supports individuals who might be struggling. Her coaching helps them make the necessary adjustments to ensure success in their organizations. She has found that in order for

SHE *Marcia*

her coaching to be effective, each individual must be eager to embrace change. The majority of her coaching clients are women, although she has also assisted men to become better versions of themselves within the work environment. Marcia also enjoys facilitating workshops and meetings. She has developed subject matter which she presents primarily to management. These topics are specific and tailored to each organization.

The decision to become a full-time consultant and coach was a natural transition. Her many years of leadership with Mutual of New York (MONY), in both human resources and information technology, followed by corporate positions at Seton Family of Hospitals and the Ascension system, gave her a deep background in how companies position themselves through their human resources departments. MONY was designated as one of the 100 Best Companies by Working Mother magazine for three years running, and Seton received the honor as a Best Place to Work in Austin three times—all while Marcia was leading the charge in the people business. The former chief operating officer of Seton Healthcare described Marcia as "having the knowledge of the full range of human resource issues faced by a large organization, a wise consistency that treated people fairly and recognized when a situation required a different approach, openness to new programs and methods and a team player." These attributes hold Marcia in good stead as she heads up programs that not only support departments and organizations, but also bring out the best in leaders and future leaders.

And then there's the nickname "badass."

Lisa

WEBB

Webb Jam

Lisa Webb is a self-proclaimed Type A (even A-plus-plus) personality. Success came naturally for her for over 30 years (working for others or leading her own companies). With loads of education, experience and connections, she was a dynamic mover and shaker in Austin, Texas. Those who worked or socialized with her always knew that if they needed support, they could call on Lisa, who could get things done and make big things happen. A self-starter and an enthusiastic supporter in the political arena, Lisa was tireless and committed. Starting her own business was natural. In fact, she has launched several.

In the blink of an eye, things can change. In 2015, while helping her mom move a garbage bin to the curb, fate set Lisa on a different course. An unstable rolling garbage bin, a strong gust of wind, and Lisa found herself flipping through the air to land on her head on a concrete driveway. Her professional trajectory was about to change.

The result was a traumatic brain injury, which affected every facet of her life. Along with physical issues such as persistent nausea and sensitivity to light and sound, she felt a shift in her driven Type A personality.

SHE *Lisa*

Neuroscientist and author Dr. Jill Bolte Taylor, who suffered a brain injury due to a stroke, discovered that while some areas of the brain are incapacitated and fail to function as in the past, for her, other areas flourished and blossomed. Although there was full physical recovery over time, new talents emerged. This was also the case for Lisa Webb, and it changed the course of her personal and business interests. Neuropsychologists agree that a change of personality is not unusual with traumatic brain injuries. The brain accommodates itself and often uncovers new talents.

In order to understand the origin of the drive within any entrepreneur, it is important to examine their roots. Lisa began life in El Campo, Texas, the daughter of parents who were very involved in her upbringing and development. Her entrepreneurial spirit came from her dad, who, as a salesman of office supplies, made the move to open his own office supply store. As one of five children, Lisa spent a lot of time in the small-town office supply business environment. At the age of three, she was fully engaged in the business, with her own desk and chair near that of her dad.

The "Ozzie and Harriet" life came to an abrupt halt when her dad passed away at the age of 40. Lisa's mom became the head of the household, tasked with a business to run and extensive family real estate to manage. Lisa was able to benefit from a large amount of her childhood spent with an aunt and uncle, who were homebuilders and additional inspirations toward creating one's own business.

As Lisa entered the University of Texas at Austin, she chose a social science composite degree and also began working at the State Capitol as a Senate messenger. The heady world of politics and the influencers who inhabited it were a perfect arena for the capable and accomplished Lisa. Betty King, the beloved Secretary of the Senate who ran the show in and out of session, recognized Lisa's talents and shepherded her into a significant position with the Texas Education Agency, where she worked for three years overseeing compliance in school districts.

Lisa's skills in getting the job done prompted a call from a colleague running for office. She wanted Lisa's expertise on her campaign for a run at a Senate seat. This role, plus a subsequent role on the election team of Ann Richards, governor of Texas, and oversight of the inauguration, called into play all of Lisa's organizational and people skills. Lisa remained involved in politics after Governor Richards' election and inauguration. Working closely with a colleague, Lisa continued to provide consulting and support for educational agencies until she made the decision to pursue a master's degree in psychological counseling. She opened a private practice in her hometown of El Campo, then moved her practice back to Austin and included executive coaching and development—something that was second nature to Lisa. For nearly a decade, Lisa guided a small group of large corporate clients, as well as individuals. Then in 2015, Lisa made one of her frequent trips to El Campo to visit her mom. The simple task of taking out the garbage became the life (and career) changer.

After the concussion, Lisa could not continue working with clients at Lisa Webb Consulting and spent months focusing on healing and recovery. Sensitivity to light and sound meant a life in dark, quiet locations, for the most part. As Lisa began to recover, she had a sense of beautiful imagery and that she needed to capture these vivid pictures on canvas. Painting was not one of her known talents, but suddenly, she was compelled to create … and create she did. She not only learned to express herself through stunning art, but also she and a newly hired assistant created a website to support concussion victims and their families through education and networking. In this way, she was able to utilize her creative mind and her background of support and counseling to help those who had experienced a similar injury.

But she was not done. In 2017, as she continued to paint images and ideas that were becoming frequent inspiration to her shifting consciousness, she began to turn a dream of global positivity into a reality via Webb Digital Network. WDN is the parent company of Webb Jam, a digital platform for upbeat, inspirational and educational stories. Lisa was inspired to create this platform after being overwhelmed with negative daily news. The site provides positive, fun and educational information from Lisa's staff but also accepts submissions from outside authors. The network went live in 2020. Now Webb Jam exists to build community in a positive way with positive messages. All of it was created by a Type A, driven entrepreneur who discovered talents beyond what she imagined.

Carolyn
SIMPSON WELLS

Dance By Design Studios

Ms. Carolyn's enthusiasm and love for dance shows in her face and her voice when she talks about her two dance studio locations and hundreds of students. The effervescence critical to the success of a dancer also lives in Carolyn as a studio owner and teacher. Each day is a nonstop whirlwind of family, business development, staff leadership, dance costumes and shoes, event planning and children's smiling faces as they dance and whirl through exercises and routines developed especially for them. Dance By Design Studios in New Braunfels, Texas, is the icing on the dance cake that has been baked over the past two decades.

As a child growing up in Georgia, Carolyn was one of three daughters who were all encouraged by their parents to do and be anything they chose, and she committed fully to the goal. Dancing since the age of 3, Carolyn took classes throughout childhood, eventually dancing 20-25 hours per week while in high school. Continuing her love of dance into college, she attended the University of Georgia, majoring in dance education. Although she primarily studied ballet and modern dance, she also found time outside of school to spend off hours with a ballroom dancing group. After graduation, Carolyn joined Ad Deum dance company in Houston, where she initially taught part time, transitioning to full time. After leaving Ad Deum, she began travels as a performer with the Holland America cruise line. Required to perform only three

SHE *Carolyn*

days per week, she spent the balance of her time helping other staff on board or participating in excursions at the ports of call (from Alaska to Antarctica). Carolyn was always moving, always busy. The contracts with Holland America were eight months in length, so with a few months "on leave" rather than sitting still, Carolyn performed with the Radio City Rockettes during the Christmas season. With eight months performing at sea and four months with the Rockettes, Carolyn's year was booked. For two years, she lived in and out of New York, dancing and auditioning and dancing some more.

After five years of performing on the road or sea and holiday seasons in New York, Carolyn returned to Georgia to put down some roots, acquiring a dog, a car and a house that needed some renovation. Never one to be still for long, she took a summer to travel the U.S., teaching dance at Air Force bases, before completing one more season as a Rockette. With her house nearing rehab completion, her dog happily reunited with her, and a car in use, Carolyn found love next. Eager to continue teaching, when she was called back to Houston to Ad Deum, she responded to the call. When her new love proposed and they were married, they relocated to New Braunfels and started their family. Having put down roots, Carolyn began to bring into reality a lifelong dream of owning and operating her own dance studio and providing dance education.

Carolyn's focus has always been on a wholesome, family-oriented dance education for all ages. She promises appropriate music, choreography and costumes and an environment where all students and teaching staff feel safe,

secure and appreciated. She stresses that they learn proper technique,
discipline and a love of dance to last a lifetime. She pays special attention to
every detail of the experience. She asks the questions, "Is the music uplifting?" "Are the lyrics appropriate?" "Do the costumes make the dancers
feel positively about their bodies and do not exploit them?" Above all, in
a teacher/child environment where children often do not feel they have
the power to see something/say something, she asks, "Does everyone
understand positive role modeling and what constitutes a safe and loving
environment?" In a world where instructors and teachers often misuse
their power and authority over little ones, Ms. Carolyn wants to be 100%
sure that her studios are wholesome, safe and secure for all.

The Dance By Design Studios do not have competitive teams but rather
performance teams. Unfortunately, competition occasionally brings out

a negative aspect in dance, which Carolyn wants to avoid. Performances by classes and groups include everyone performing at their best and enjoying the experience, rather than working toward "beating out" their fellow team members. She leaves competition to other studios. Her children and teens experience the discipline and the love of dance without the pressure to win. All of these aspects of dance education bring her joy. In addition, she and her staff seek to find the style that suits a child the best. While a youngster may seem to hate one style, another suits them to a T, and that brings both the child and Ms. Carolyn joy. Her goal is to create moments and memories while protecting her kids from any harm.

Carolyn has found that having mentors in a business forum is critical to her success. Although many women in business do not seek out a mentor until they are in their mid-to-late 40s, and 63% of women in the workforce have never had a mentor, Carolyn knows the value of having at least one. Also, 78% of women in current businesses indicate that they act as mentors for at least one other person in some manner; however, very few of them had mentors of their own. As more women become business owners and leaders, the value of mentorship is obvious. Carolyn credits her virtual group of dance academy owners with providing support and advice during times of success and times of challenge.

At the end of a nonstop day, which has been a part of a nonstop week, Carolyn stresses that she wants to provide joy, discipline, technique, safety and, above all, kindness.

Dr. Aisha
WHITE

Quintessence Plastic Surgery

As a child growing up in New Orleans, Aisha White did not fit the stereotype (if there is one) of a future plastic surgeon with a master's in business administration. She was whip smart with a love of science and a family of elders who encouraged her to pursue whatever dream she could dream. Although she comes from a long line of intelligent, strong women, Aisha is aware of the influence the men in her family had on her. They believed she could be or do anything. When her dad and grandpa learned that, as an eighth grade student, she wanted to be a doctor, these progressive men were supportive, knew she was capable and told her so.

Although the journey to becoming a doctor is a structured one, Aisha knew from an early age that she always wanted to be open to possibilities and potential opportunities as they presented themselves. At the age of 16, many young girls are thinking of things other than education; however, Aisha was different. She entered Howard University, majoring in microbiology. A gap year in France preceded her acceptance into the Feinberg School of Medicine at Northwestern University. Understanding the importance of the business side of a medical practice, Aisha concurrently attended the Wharton School of Business, receiving an MBA. She ultimately completed her internship and residency in General Surgery at SUNY Health Science Center, followed by a residency in plastic surgery at the University of Illinois in Chicago.

At the beginning of her medical education, she was open to all special-ties. She ultimately chose plastic surgery because she enjoyed the creative aspect, plus she embraced the opportunity to make a permanent impact on individuals' lives and self-esteem. Although practicing male physi-cians of all specialties outnumber women 64% to 36%, the trend is changing. For the past 10 years, the number of women entering medi-cal school has been climbing. The number of women in medicine has increased by almost double the number of their male counterparts. The number of female doctors currently under the age of 35 is a little more than half of the total in this age group. The gender imbalance is changing. In plastic surgery, where the patient population is 90% women, only 10% of the surgeons are women. Aisha White is clearly one of the few who was open to the possibility of choosing differently. Her passion for people and relationships led to a career in medicine and also pointed the way to her specialty.

Aisha's approach to patients is unique in that she believes plastic surgery is not about changing people but helping them become their best self as they are. She focuses on body positivity and enhancements as well as reconstruction. After initially joining a plastic surgery practice as the sole female physician, she made the decision to launch her own practice, soon to celebrate its 10th birthday. Her practice is called Quintessence, which means the purest and most concentrated essence of a substance. She believes that anyone's aesthetic treatment plan should be customized for their specific goals. In this way, the focus is not on physical perfection but on personal feelings of empowerment.

Any business can be stressful, and ownership of a medical practice can be doubly so. Aisha works to maintain work/life balance. Journaling is not only a stress reliever but also an opportunity to express her thoughts and dreams in a form available only to her. Writing to express personal thoughts and goals allows her to have an active brain dump without judgment. The underlying theme of her journal entries is gratitude, which has been medically proven to rewire the brain and enhance life. Gratitude has been found to unshackle individuals from negative emotions. Research shows health benefits from expressing gratitude privately through writing without ever sharing it with anyone.

In addition to her gratitude practice, physical activity is a must. A swimming pool is her home away from home. When not in the office or operating room, Aisha can be found counting laps and eliminating stress. Swimming laps is a spiritual experience for her, centering her and allowing for clarity in strategic planning and thinking. Studies indicate that mental ability is directly linked to physical activity. And nowhere are the implications more relevant than to performance at work. Cognitive benefits include improved concentration, sharper memory, faster learning, prolonged mental stamina, enhanced creativity and lower stress. These are important in any work environment, especially when business ownership is a part of life.

In addition to activities that benefit Aisha individually, she also has served on the board of directors of Ballet Austin and Vivent Health and is chair of the Diversity, Equity and Inclusion Committee of the Department of Surgery at Dell Medical School at the University of Texas. She has been featured in the Austin Black Business Journal as a member of the Top 10 Black Physicians, was a finalist in the Austin Business Journal Profiles in Power and makes time for volunteer commitments. She is an alumnus of Leadership Austin and an active member of Junior League of Austin. Volunteering keeps Aisha grounded and also grateful.

Aisha provides an avenue for women to be the physical best that they choose to be through plastic surgery, and she has also shared advice in women's publications on suggested solutions for women with health struggles. She advises women to give themselves the time to heal, explore all resources and ask for help and support. She is an advocate of taking mental breaks from stressors and being open to possibilities to just *be* without self-sabotage. Health and beauty starts from within.

Dr. Angie
WHITWORTH

West Lynn Veterinary Clinic

Dr. Angie Whitworth is an "Aggie," meaning she attended Texas A&M University. Its home, College Station, Texas, is a long way from Australia where Angie was born and spent her early years growing up and being "mom" to her adopted kitty Misty. After a move to Singapore, her love of animals was played out in the local wet markets, defending the baby bunnies from taunts by other children and being an informal overseer of the small pets at the petting zoo, ensuring that all of the animals living there received kind treatment. Angie moved to the U.S. to attend the University of Arizona, obtaining a bachelor's degree in agriculture in the pre-veterinary program. She was especially drawn to genetic engineering and briefly considered that as a career before settling on veterinary medicine.

After graduation from the University of Arizona, Angie relocated to Austin, Texas, where she worked in the real estate industry before applying to veterinary medical school at Texas A&M, the only veterinary school in the state. Following graduation, she moved back to Austin and worked as a small-animal practitioner until she purchased West Lynn Veterinary Clinic in 2011. She and her husband have three children, and Angie has her hands full, as do many female business owners.

SHE Dr. Angie

Parent entrepreneurs have double responsibilities to their businesses and to their families; finding ways to devote time to both is key to achieving that elusive work-life balance. Often this means the best solution is to leave the employ of another and start one's own business. Working for others often requires making difficult choices. The culture of the work world is shifting a bit to allow women more flexibility, but working for yourself often allows more freedom than working for someone else. According to the Pew Research Center, mothers with children are three times as likely as fathers to say that being a parent made it difficult for them to have a business or career and a family. Angie acknowledges that juggling family life, practicing medicine and running a small business requires her to be ever-present. Although there was an option to register for business courses while in medical school, Angie had not anticipated owning a business so didn't pursue any of the classes offered. Finding support and resources is never easy for small businesses; however, she has sought out a specialty business group that has helped to navigate the business side of her successful practice.

Angie is fortunate to have other female associates on staff at WLVC. Dr. Taylor Smithee graduated with a bachelor's degree from Texas A&M University before completing her Doctor of Veterinary Medicine from the same school. She worked as a general practice veterinarian for a few years before joining the team at West Lynn. Privately owned small animal clinics are difficult to find now, and she wanted to join a family-friendly atmosphere, which she found in West Lynn. Not only her love of animals, but her desire to help the people who owned the animals motivated her to become a veterinarian. She was encouraged by her parents to work in a veterinary clinic while in high school to learn if the career path would be a good fit. She knows that most people believe individuals become veterinarians because they like animals, but she feels that it is the people who own the pets who mean the most to her. Making pet owners happy with their treatment and the care of their pets is important to her, and she never tires of talking to them about their fur babies. All of the hard work is totally worth it, although she still needs to find time to care for herself when possible. Relaxing and recharging through yoga and quiet time are essential for her.

Dr. Dalied Rodriguez has always loved animals. Growing up in Puerto Rico, she knew from a young age what her career path would be. After

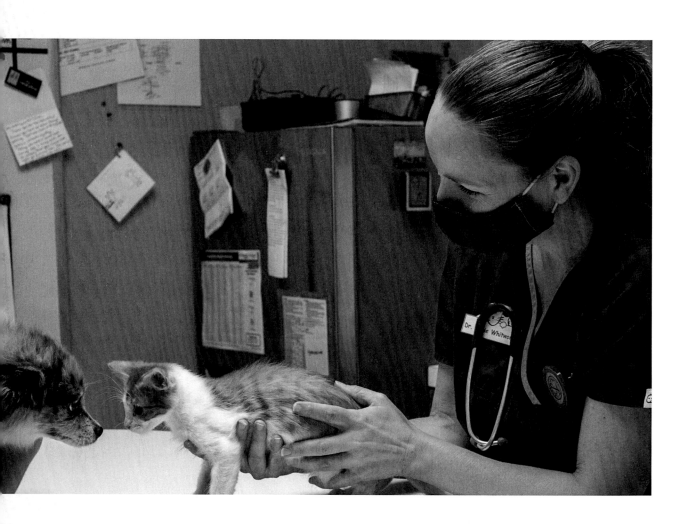

receiving her DVM from Ross University, she returned to San Juan where she worked briefly before returning to the U.S. to complete internships in Los Angeles, then Austin. She has been with West Lynn for over three years and has developed a special interest in surgery and emergency care. She credits her family—her mom, dad and sister—as the best support system a person could have. They encouraged her through medical school and entry into the practice. Although she believes that women are extremely well-suited to medicine due to their gentleness, kindness and good instincts, she believes that men as well as women possess these qualities. She loves her work and feels fulfilled at the end of each day, knowing she has helped so many pets to better health and helped their owners feel good about the care.

The fourth member of the team at WLVC is Dr. Elizabeth Ashbaugh, who was born and raised in Austin. After graduating from the University of Texas, she received her DVM from Texas A&M University. After working in Colorado at a small animal clinic and in Austin as an emergency veterinarian, she joined West Lynn. Having known clinic owner Angie in veterinarian school, Elizabeth knew that she would be a good fit for the clinic. She found that the care team truly cares for the pets and their owners. Like her colleagues at the clinic, Elizabeth knows that caring for the concerns and needs of the owner is just as important as the care of the pet. Serving owners during challenging times and celebrating with them during the good events is a plus. Connecting and working together with pet parents to develop a treatment plan is such a positive experience and makes the work and emotional part of the practice well worth the effort. As a general practice veterinarian, she is able to develop long-term relationships with owners and their pets, and she finds this extremely gratifying. As a female practitioner (55% of veterinarians are female), Elizabeth believes that women are exceptionally suited to the profession because of the unique combination of compassion and complex problem-solving ability.

As more women continue to apply to veterinary schools, the field will see more women working in private practice and heading up their own clinics. Significant reasons for women to select this career path include helping animals and owners, engaging in challenging work, making an excellent salary, solving problems, enjoying professional independence, participating in lifetime learning and discovering extensive career opportunities. Flexible schedules are another draw for those who balance their work life with family or personal pursuits.

The four doctors of West Lynn Veterinary Clinic provide the best of compassionate care that all pet owners desire for their fur babies. Clinic owner Dr. Angie Whitworth shoulders the common worries of managing a business and medical practice while balancing family and work life, but at the end of the day, she stays focused on the clients she loves who entrust their four-legged family members to her staff. Working for the best health outcomes for all is the common goal while ensuring that the clinic is efficient, well-run and successful.

SHE *Dr. Angie*

Vanessa

WILKERSON

Ace Custom Tailors

Brooklyn-born Vanessa Wilkerson can trace her love of fashion to her early years and endless days of dressing and accessorizing Barbies. She considers herself highly intuitive when it comes to knowledge of clothing, its design and fit. That, coupled with intense curiosity, led her to read and learn everything she could in the stacks of magazines found in her childhood home.

A move from New York to Chicago with her mom led her to a new home and new stepfamily that she adored. The male members of the family were musicians, and music filled her house, jam sessions providing a background of jazz music to accompany her young years. A subsequent move back to New York City and old neighborhoods provided Vanessa with the opportunity to become involved in the hip-hop culture. As she developed her dance style, she was also building a reputation as a fashionista. Working as an intern in the wardrobe department of several movies, Vanessa was an energetic and fast learner. By asking questions and showing an eagerness to work hard, she landed her jobs on multiple movie sets during her school years.

After graduation from high school, Vanessa enrolled in the Fashion Institute of Technology, a public college in Manhattan. FIT is part of the State University of New York and focuses on art, business, design,

SHE

Vanessa

mass communication and technology connected to the fashion industry. Vanessa's drive to learn kept the faculty one short step ahead of her. She swamped them with questions and sought every challenge. Sewing rooms at FIT became a second home to her. Fashion design, styling and costume design occupied only a part of her time as she continued to intern on movies and videos.

Falling in love and a marriage brought her to Austin, Texas, where her eagerness and enthusiasm for fashion and creating gorgeous designs grew. Vanessa relocated from New York to Texas and brought her flair for design and wardrobe construction with her. Although she initially considered enrolling in a university fashion degree program, she ultimately decided to do what she did best: work hard, learn everything she could in the fashion industry and get ahead.

Vanessa learned all she could about the few custom tailoring companies in Austin and believed that Ace Custom Tailors would be a good fit. This award-winning company was (and still is) the largest, most highly recognized tailor shop in Texas. Their mission was (and still is) to provide exceptional quality tailoring with superior service. Vanessa believed she had found her professional home.

Tailors design and make new clothing, but they also take ill-fitting items and transform them into perfectly fitted shirts, pants and dresses for all body types. This miraculous makeover requires a practiced eye and trained hands. It is estimated that there are approximately 34,000

SHE Vanessa

individuals who work as tailors in the U.S. Some of the professionals work independently, but most work for clothing stores, department stores or specialty tailoring businesses such as Ace Custom Tailors. Each of the employees typically serves apprenticeships for many years under the direction of master tailors.

In choosing Ace, Vanessa wanted to start at an entry level in order to learn the business. She began as an entry-level fitter and was promoted over time, first to fitting consultant, then to master tailor and then to director of operations for all of the Ace operations and locations. As the leader of all staff and operations, she acquired shares of ownership as her tenure increased. Earning ownership in a business via years of service is a unique path to ownership that Vanessa enjoys.

It is not uncommon for business owners to be without business degrees or business experience. Prior to starting their businesses more than half of all U.S. owners do not have a background in the financial side of a business. This supports the view that a business degree is not a prerequisite to the success of a company. Most owners who have all of the technical expertise necessary to grow a certain type of business typically rely on others to provide the support or training in order to sustain profitability and growth. Vanessa has been mentored by management staff and ownership throughout her promotions, and just as she quickly absorbed the technical training at FIT, she has immersed herself in the numbers side of the business, which drives the company toward growth and success.

One of Vanessa's superpowers is her passion and talent for tailoring wedding attire. Intricately made bridal gowns and alterations, custom fittings, rush orders and out-of-the-ordinary requests are her cup of tea. Discouraged brides with ill-fitting gowns are often directed to Vanessa to make the magic happen. And she does. Time and time again, she skillfully takes those chosen dream dresses from frumpy to fabulous and from baggy to bodacious. Her goal is for her clients to fall in love with what she creates or renovates. She knows that when a garment fits well, the wearer feels beautiful. Wedding attire is her jam.

Vanessa has also utilized her skills in creating and producing costumes for Austin Lyric Opera and Zachary Scott Theater, both well-known Austin institutions. Anyone who has had a chance to attend shows at these two venues knows that the costuming is elaborate and a major enhancement to each production. With each costume and each unusual fitting for each performer, Vanessa has increased her expertise in challenging tailoring.

Ace Custom Tailors has thrived under the leadership of Vanessa Wilkerson. The first quarter of 2020 was one of the most successful on record for the multiple locations, following two years of already strong growth. The numbers were up, and bridal season was on the horizon. And then, as has occurred for every business globally, a pandemic came to visit the shops. Keeping employees on payroll—and safe—was essential. Although the business closed fully during mandatory closures, as soon as it was permissible, employees returned and began to construct masks to fill the need in the medical community. The staff of Ace Custom Tailors became mask makers. By the end of the urgent call for masks from University of Texas Health, over 80,000 had been made and delivered by Ace Tailors. As the local Austin community began to reopen and lives moved back to a more regular pace, business returned. There were garments to construct and wedding dresses to magically transform. And the skilled eye of Vanessa and the hands of her professional staff ensure that customers continue to fall in love with the clothing that has been created just for them.

Diana
ZUNIGA

Investors Alliance

Diana Zuniga is founder and president of Investors Alliance, a full-service commercial real estate company that provides income property brokerage, leasing and asset disposition services, site acquisition and development and a dozen other services valued by the commercial real estate community in Austin, Texas. None of these services were part of Diana's master plan unfolding in Laredo, Texas, as the oldest of 10 children. With a work ethic modeled by her parents and grandparents, Diana has only known the focused life of hard work and the drive to get ahead while always doing the right thing. Family involvement in school, work, church and community were a way of life for the Zuniga clan. Staying focused, committed and busy were her strengths. Dedication to getting the job done has always been all Diana knew.

After receiving her degree from the University of Texas at Austin, Diana founded the Hyline Dance Team at the newly opened Westlake High School in Austin. As a former Kilgore Rangerette, and with the drive to take on any large task, she was perfectly suited to establish an organization that still continues decades later. After two years in this role, she felt the tug to pursue her dream as a professional dancer in Los Angeles. It was during her time in California that she began to work in real estate, buying and selling houses. When family and home called her back to Texas, she and her husband returned, and she quickly earned her real estate license and set to work. The couple added a son to their family a year later.

Starting out in residential real estate, Diana quickly determined that the commercial market was her primary interest. Beginning with small deals, she quickly became known as a persistent and pleasant representative for both buyers and sellers. Her ability to listen carefully and seek to understand caused her star in the commercial market to quickly rise. Her innate work ethic and straight-shooting style made her a popular deal-maker. As she has often said, she didn't know that the business and making deals was supposed to be hard, she just kept "doing it" and relying on her instincts. Although she was one of the very few women in commercial real estate in Austin, Diana never felt the pinch of discrimination. As one of 10 children, she had long ago learned to stay prepared and show up ready for any conversation or situation. Male or female colleagues made no difference. She showed up, and she performed in ways long ingrained in her personality.

Unlike Diana, nearly half (42%) of women indicate that they have felt some sort of gender bias in their interactions in business. This may range from overt harassment to subtle looks or insinuations. Some women experience discrimination in pay scale, which has been reported as 82% of what male counterparts earn in the same position. Diana Zuniga experienced none of this. Her expectations were always that she would work hard and be treated fairly and paid well. These expectations were always met.

Diana partnered with a local real estate colleague between 1992-1996, when she founded her own company, Investors Alliance, specializing in multifamily sales. At that time, she purchased land and an industrial building in the downtown Austin area, which was home to several small businesses and artists. Investors Alliance had offices in this building until 2007, when ground was broken on Austin's first point tower (a strikingly tall and slender building that melds skyscraper and high-rise residence) condominium project. In partnership with three others, Diana developed the 42-story building, which, at the time, was the eighth tallest building

in the downtown area. The first homes were sold in 2009. Through hard work and believing that nothing can hold her back, Diana has become a part of the 4% of women in real estate firms who "touch the money" and have significant decision-making power. Because she never subscribed to the belief that the development process would be difficult, she excelled. All of the units in her Spring Condominium project have been sold, and Diana is on to the next project. Her latest is a five-story, 120,983-square-foot office building in downtown Austin. It broke ground in early 2020. And in her true fashion with grit and determination, she will deliver a successful project—along with a development partner who started his career in Austin while working as Diana's intern at UT. She mentored him well, and the pair will now deliver a Class A office building in 2021. Her young development partner learned that there is only one way to conduct business and that is the right way, never taking shortcuts. He attributes his success to what he learned from Diana, who taught him to go the extra mile for clients and be willing to do whatever it takes, even if it is not your direct responsibility.

Examples of women mentoring men are scarce, and most often, stories are written about the importance of women and their impact on other women. Currently, there is much written on the value of male allies. Programs placing men in the role of boosters of women do not tell the whole story. Many women such as Diana Zuniga embody qualities that can make good leaders great. The narrative of mentorship only going in one direction can reinforce a negative bias about men as role models for women. There are examples of women mentorship programs in corporate America; however, these stories don't receive a lot of notice. Mentors such as Diana, who exemplifies strength of character, work ethic and a spirit of preparedness, are ideally suited for this role. Her intelligence, gift of collaboration, communication and empathy are especially valuable in the space of a male-dominated profession such as commercial real estate. As her current business partner says, she is additive in everything she touches and leads with passion and integrity.

Hard work and the willingness to continue learning new things keep her perspective fresh and open to possibilities around every corner. And Diana has more goals: living life to the fullest and delivering a quality project. Oh yes, and learning how to do a 360-degree spin on a wakeboard. Given her track record, she will do it all.

Resources

At Last

Stacy Francis, "11 tips for 11 million women – how female entrepreneurs can beat the odds," CNBC, October 21, 2019, https://www.cnbc.com/2019/10/21/how-todays-11-million-female-entrepreneurs-can-beat-the-odds.

Sam Dimitriu, "What do the next generation of entrepreneurs really think?" Elite Business Magazine, August 29, 2019, http://elitebusinessmagazine.co.uk/analysis/item/what-do-the-next-generation-of-entrepreneurs-really-think.

Maddie Shepherd, "17 Women-Owned Business Stats You Need to Know," Fundera, December 16, 2020, https://www.fundera.com/resources/women-owned-business-statistics.

"Women Entrepreneurs Less Likely to Seek and Obtain Financing than Men," PRNewswire, May 10, 2018, https://www.prnewswire.com/news-releases/women-entrepreneurs-less-likely-to-seek-and-obtain-financing-than-men.

Matt Mansfield, "STARTUP STATISTICS – The Numbers You Need to Know," Small Business Trends, March 28, 2019, https://smallbiztrends.com/2019/03/startup-statistics-small-business.

"Women Business Owner Statistics," NAWBO, accessed March 10, 2021, https://www.nawbo.org/resources/women-business-owner-statistics.

Carmen Davailus

Carmen Davailus Buck, "Just See Me" (Bloomington, Indiana: Balboa Press, 2018), p. xiv.

Nelly Garcia

United States Congress Joint Economic Committee Democrats, "JEC, CHC Release New Report on the Economic State of the Hispanic Community and Why Hispanics are Key to the Nation's Recovery," Chairman Rep. Don Beyer (D-VA), September 30, 2020, https://www.jec.senate.gov/public/index.cfm/democrats/press-releases.

Guadalupe Gonzalez, "The Number of Latinx-Run Startups Is Rocketing. Their Funding Is Not. Here's Why That's a Big Problem," Inc. Magazine, March/April 2020, https://www.inc.com/magazine/202004/guadalupe-gonzalez/latinx-hispanic-entrepreneur-funding-loan-gap-opportunity-scale-economy.html.

Lindsey Hohlt

Paula Fernandes and Marisa Sanfilippo, "Challenges Faced by Women Entrepreneurs and Some of the Most Successful Women to Follow," Business News Daily, June 2020, https://www.businessnewsdaily.com/5268-women-entrepreneur-challenges.

Rieva Lesonsky, "The State of Women Entrepreneurs," SCORE, March 24, 2020, https://www.score.org/blog/state-women-entrepreneurs.

Sandra Hutchens and Jamie Klingenberg

Susan Ward, "Why Business Partnerships Fail," The Balance Small Business, January 29, 2020, https://www.thebalancesmb.com/why-business-partnerships-fail.

LaToncia (Dee) Jones

"Stimulating Facts About Coffee," How Stuff Works, updated February 20, 2021, https://recipes.howstuffworks.com/coffee-facts.

Allegra Kavugh

Katie Psencik, "Austin has third-highest rate of pet ownership in U.S., survey says," Austin360/ Austin American-Statesman, updated September 23, 2018, https://www.austin360.com/entertainment/20170407/

austin-has-third-highest-rate-of-pet-ownership-in-us-survey-says.

Pam LeBlanc

Elaine Pofeldt, "Full-time Freelancing Lures More
Americans," Forbes.com, October 5, 2019, https://
www.forbes.com/sites/elainepofeldt/2019/10/05/
full-time-freelancing-lures-more-americans.

Carmaleta McKinnis-Williams

Jeanette Settembre, "Women who have female role models are more
likely to value their worth," MarketWatch, June 6, 2018, https://www.
marketwatch.com/story/women-who-have-female-role-models-are-
more-likely-to-value-their-worth-2018-06-06.

Aditi Merchant

2016 BNP Paribas Global Entrepreneur Report, "The
Emergence of the 'Millennipreneur,'" BNP Paribas,
accessed May 26, 2021, https://group.bnpparibas/en/news/
bnp-paribas-global-entrepreneurs-report-2016.

Lisa Firestone, Ph.D., "Why Millennials are So Lonely," Psychology
Today, September 18, 2019, https://www.psychologytoday.com/us/
blog/compassion-matters/201909/why-millennials-are-so-lonely.

Cassie Shankman

"Women in Male Dominated Industries and Occupations: A Quick Take," Catalyst, February 5, 2020, https://www.catalyst.org/research/women-in-male-dominated-industries-and-occupations.

Marcia Silverberg

"The Megaphone of Main Street: Women's Entrepreneurship, Spring 2018," SCORE, April 23, 2018, https://www.score.org/resource/megaphone-main-street-women-entrepreneurs.

Carolyn Simpson Wells

Brittany Voris, "How women can find mentors in the workplace," Berkeley Haas MBA Blog, March 11, 2020, https://blogs.haas.berkeley.edu/the-berkeley-mba/how-women-can-find-mentors.

Dr. Aisha White

Amy Morin, "7 Scientifically Proven Benefits of Gratitude," Psychology Today, April 3, 2015, https://www.psychologytoday.com/us/blog/what-mentally-strong-people-dont-do/201504/7-scientifically-proven-benefits-gratitude.

Dr. Angie Whitworth

"Male vs. Female Veterinarians, "ILoveVeterinary.com, updated March 21, 2021, https://iloveveterinary.com/blog/female-vs-male-veterinary-doctors/.

Vanessa Wilkerson

Mark Juang, "A secret many small-business owners share with Mark Zuckerberg," CNBC, July 19, 2017, https://www.cnbc.com/2017/07/19/survey-shows-majority-of-business-owners-lack-college-degree.

Diana Zuniga

Kim Parker and Cary Funk, "Gender discrimination comes in many forms for today's working women," Pew Research Center, December 14, 2017, https://www.pewresearch.org/fact-tank/2017/12/14/gender-discrimination-comes-in-many-forms-for-todays-working-women/.